LETTERS TO MY CHILDREN

D055627b

LETTERS TO MY CHILDREN

Charles R. Bressler

Gatekeeper Press
Columbus, Ohio

Letters to My Children

Published by Gatekeeper Press
2167 Stringtown Rd, Suite 109
Columbus, OH 43123-2989
www.GatekeeperPress.com

Copyright © 2021 by Charles R. Bressler
All rights reserved. Neither this book, nor any parts within it may be sold or reproduced in any form or by any electronic or mechanical means, including information storage and retrieval systems without permission in writing from the author. The only exception is by a reviewer, who may quote short excerpts in a review.

The cover design and editorial work for this book are entirely the product of the author. Gatekeeper Press did not participate in and is not responsible for any aspect of these elements.

Library of Congress Control Number: 2020950707

ISBN (paperback): 9781662907609

CONTENTS

Preface

Over the years, a number of friends and family have suggested that I write a book. There are people who were somewhat familiar with my life story and suggested that they thought it might be of some interest to others. I always hesitated. First off, I wasn't sure that my life was that interesting. Secondly, the task of writing a book seemed daunting. I felt trying to write a book was going to steep me in gobs and gobs of time in which I would feel nothing had been accomplished.

Later in life, my children began to talk to me about writing a book. They complained that they didn't really know much about their Dad. After all, we had lived separately through much of their growing up. I had missed many major events in their lives. I did attend each of their high school graduations, but I missed my son's Little League games and other events in which he was a star. I missed my daughter's musical performances and other events and so I understand why they felt their father was somewhat a very distant person.

Finally, my son, who had already written a book of his own, suggested that he would help me if I would sit down and give this information. He said that he and his sister were primarily interested in learning about my early life and other areas that needed filled in as far as they were concerned. I have attempted in this document to fill in the gaps that my children have asked about. I've chosen to write this in a strange format. The book is called, "Letters to My Children," and that is exactly what it is. I take various sections of my life and put them down, sharing the highlights and other details. Hopefully, my children will get some sense of their father's character; good, bad, and indifferent.

I want to thank my son, daughter, and others for helping me with this endeavor, this project of sorts. I need to point out that the word blind as used in this book not only refers to totally blind individuals, but also those who have a visual acuity defined as legally blind. I'm sure I will have other acknowledgements as I go along. I would also like to thank my wife for her patience and support. I have several friends who have expressed an interest in reading this material. Therefore, I have decided that it is time to put it down and get the whole thing over with. I must admit that it's been quite an experience going back through memory lane remembering events and situations that were highly influential throughout my entire life. At nearly the end of my 82nd year, I feel that I have lived a long life that has been filled with experiences in which many will never be duplicated again. Blind schools now don't take on people with high academic qualifications. Those people were main streamed into the public-school systems. Blind schools are now filled with children who have multiple handicaps that don't permit them the ability or chance to go to public schools.

Blindness itself has changed a great deal over the years. Today, much of it is related to age, due to macular degeneration, Diabetes, cataracts, which are now very treatable and other infirmities. Some is due to injury, particularly among military personnel who served in various areas that are volatile and hazardous. Many of them have written very insightful books about what has happened to them. Blindness has also been helped greatly thanks to technological advancements. There are now such gadgets as barcode identifiers, money identifiers, smartphones, iPads and computers. In fact, one of my dearest friends, who is totally blind, is a computer programmer for the government and has been so for the past 30 years. Her husband, who is partially blind like me, is a tech support person for the Federal government. Whenever I have computer related questions or iPad questions, these are the first people I contact for help. Technology has been extremely kind, although much of it is unaffordable to many blind people. Unemployment is extremely high among the blind. Many live on SSI. Some do on SSDI. They are not given a chance at any kind of gainful employment even though many are probably quite capable. I have often thought that the customer service telemarketing jobs that are frequently given to people overseas could well be given to blind people in this country to help their lot in life. There are other helps for blind people today, including the Americans with Disabilities Act.

On this account, I must say to the readers that I don't like the use of the word disabled. It has a kind of finality to it; a suggestion that the disabled person is really incapable and cannot be helped in any way. I much prefer the use of handicapped. This suggests a person who is challenged by limits, but it also leaves open the possibility that these are people that can overcome or find ways around their limitations. To me, that much more accurately describes how it is with people of various handicaps or "disabilities." I hope that the experiences I share in this project will somehow help to educate the sighted world and suggest how it is for many blind and partially sighted people. I also hope that somehow there will be greater recognition of the needs that blind people and partially sighted people require.

Norman, Dick, and Martha Bressler

Introduction

Dear Cindy and Rick,

I begin this book with an introductory letter to both of you. You will find throughout this text all kinds of stories; some funny, some sad, some tragic, and some perhaps even boring, but they are an attempt to fill in the gaps that have been left from your memories and knowledge of your father. I hope that you will learn some lessons that will be useful and helpful throughout the rest of your lives. It's been quite an experience for me. In a way, it's been very therapeutic because I've had to go back through memory lane and relive all kinds of incidents; some hurtful, some happy and joyful. I've found it to be a good review for me as it has helped me firm up some of my own feelings about my life in general.

I have not spoken much about the Spiritual element of my life, but there is one. Ever since Barb and I got married, we have attended church. I went to church as a child with my parents. I remember vividly going to a little church on a mountain top near where we lived. There, I was anointed; a healing service performed by the pastor in which one is called to the Alter, kneels down and is anointed with oil while prayers are said for his or her healing. I guess there was a hope that I would regain my eyesight as a result of this. It need not be said that didn't happen. Barb and I went to church with you kids when you were small; two or three different Methodist Churches.

Barb and I are now members of an Episcopal church in a town about 11 miles from where we live where she serves as the organist, and when that doesn't work, the pianist. I serve in the church as a lay leader, which means from time to time when the preacher is absent, I get to do the service of morning prayer. I don't get to do communion or heavy-duty pastoral activities, but I can perform the overall morning prayer service. I enjoy doing that very much and I even get to give some hopefully informative sermons from time to time. The church has been good for me in many ways. I have used the church in a way that it has helped me learn and develop a growing faith.

When I review my life, I see that I have gone through many obstacles and have always come out the better for it. I have now reached a point in my life where I believe no matter what happens, I can handle most anything. In fact, you will remember in 2005 when I was life-flighted to a local hospital. The doctors felt that I was having a heart attack and indeed, I was in pretty bad shape. This was largely due to the fact that I was overmedicated with a blood pressure reducing medication. I nearly died and suddenly learned something from that experience. I reached a point in my treatment that I asked the doctor, "Do you think I'm having a heart attack?" I heard him mention those very sobering words. He said yes and that he thought I was in the middle of one. The funniest feeling came over me at that point. I laid there relaxed and said to myself, "Well, if I'm in the middle of one I should be on the downhill side." I then thought and realized I don't have any control over this, so whatever happens, happens.

Of course, I didn't die, but I did learn an interesting lesson; Dying is something we do all the time. From the time we begin to live, we begin to die. Crossing over from this side to whatever doesn't seem very difficult at all. It's living that is very difficult. Dying can happen in an instant. It can even happen for people that don't know it's coming. I'm reminded of a line from an old Clint Eastwood movie, "The Outlaw Josey Wales," in which Clint Eastwood said to the chief of the Indians who were about to attack, "Dying is not difficult for men like you or me, it's living that's hard." I think he was quite correct.

Two significant changes in my life occurred as a result of this illness. First, I quit smoking cold turkey. I learned something about addiction, namely addiction can be broken if the person finally realizes that what he is doing is killing him. I'm not saying that quitting is easy, but I was much more motivated because of my fear of death. Secondly, I discovered that people who fear anything such as heights, or being closed in, or storms, or aloneness, really all fear death. Death is the logical extreme of virtually any fear. So, as you read this book, this collection of letters for my children, I hope you will learn some life lessons that will be beneficial to you. God Bless and thank you.

Dick's 80th Birthday hug from his kids

Chapter 1: In the Beginning...

July 19, 1938 was a Tuesday, and it was hot. The nation was just coming out of the throws of the Great Depression. My parents were 22 and 20 and were expecting their first child. They piled into my dad's 1934 Maroon colored Chevrolet and drove the 16 miles to the little town of Mill Hall to the home of my Uncle and Aunt: William and Bernice Shoemaker. Bernice was my mom's oldest sister. This is where I was born. I was the first of three boys. My mother recalls that I was not a pretty baby. She described me as the ugliest baby she had ever seen. I had a pointed head, elongated nose, long legs, a skinny frame, and in most other ways, not beautiful. After a few days at my Aunt's house, we came back to our home in the Valley.

Eight weeks later, my mother was holding me on her lap when suddenly, I threw what mom described as a convulsion, later identified as a seizure. My mother said that I had at least 19 seizures in the span of one day. When she witnessed and experienced me having the first seizure, she picked me up holding me high above her head and ran to her mother-in-law's house nearby screaming that her child was dead. Of course, I was not dead. My grandmother reassured her. After the continuous seizures, I was taken to the hospital and placed into isolation. My parents were not permitted to see or visit me. They were not allowed to feed me or have any type of contact with me. Several days passed and my parents waited to see what was going to happen. I recovered and was sent home with my parents. The doctors concluded the baby formula my parents were feeding me disagreed with me. I was placed on an alternative formula. My mother recalled I remained very sickly for some time.

At the age of four months, my parents were concerned. I did not seem to be responding. I startled easily, especially when somebody touched me. Most of the time I laid on my back in a cradle next to my cousin who was three days older than I. I didn't seem aware of my surroundings. My Aunt Mable, a dear sweet woman, although not very bright, she had a heart as big as gold. She had a brother who was totally blind and was familiar with blind people. She said to my mother, "I think your baby cannot see." Aunt Mable lit a match, placed it in front of me, moved the match back and forth, and waited to see if my eyes followed it. They did not. This convinced Aunt Mable even more that I was not able to see.

My parents took me to the hospital. I was examined by one of the local ophthalmologists and he confirmed that I was totally blind. The ophthalmologist came to my parents and said, "We have a choice. Your child is totally blind. We can do surgery and perhaps return his sight, or at least some of it, but there is a great risk." I was diagnosed with congenital cataracts. The ophthalmologist continued to explain that the operation involved poking the lens of the eye with a needle therefore making small holes so that the acid behind the eye would eat away the cataracts. The risk was that the eyeball could hemorrhage, which meant no sight, but also no eye. My parents decided that if they did nothing, I would remain totally blind for the rest of my life. If they did something and it didn't work, I would remain totally blind for the rest of my life. Essentially, they felt they had a 50/50 chance of my gaining some sight and decided to risk the procedure.

Over the next year, I received seven operations: four on the left eye and three on the right eye. Each operation involved some needling of the lens of my eyes so that the acid would eat away at the cataracts without destroying my eyes entirely. I did receive what doctors later said approximately 10% of normal vision corrected with very thick glasses. I was taken from being a totally blind infant to a partially sighted child. This was quite difficult for my parents. I couldn't exactly perform or play with other children under normal circumstances. They had to watch when I tried to walk or run anywhere. They had to be very careful that I did not trip or run into things. They had to make sure I didn't injure myself. My glasses were tied on my face with a blue ribbon because they were very thick. I retained my little wire framed glasses and recently gave them to my son. Nothing further could be done with my eyes. Cataract surgery these days is a very minimal outpatient procedure. The person goes in, has a brief laser method, and goes home an hour or so later. Clearly, a much different procedure from what I experienced in 1938.

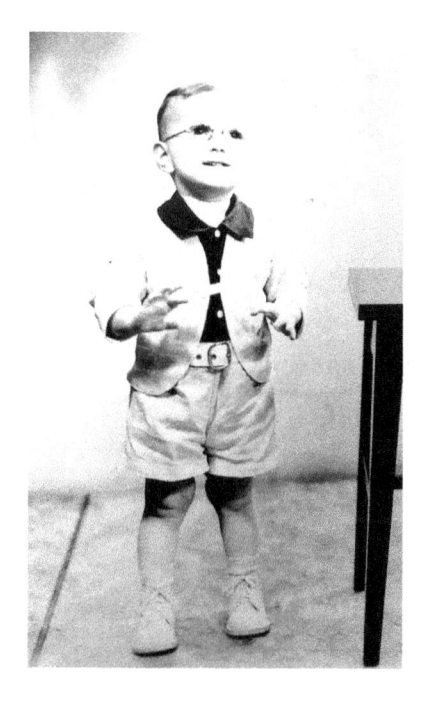

Dick as a toddler

Being bullied

Childhood as a blind person was extremely difficult for me. All the people around me had their eyesight and I was the target for getting bullied by several kids. The one bully I remember most is the neighborhood kid that always picked on me. He always picked fights. I was scared of him since I was not a fighter. He pushed and hit me. I would run to my mother crying. One occasion, I ran to my mother crying and my dad was home from work. He was annoyed and upset. He finally said to me, "If you don't go out and stand up for yourself and take your own part, I'm going to kick your ass, and it will hurt worse than anything this kid can do to you."

The time came when the kid picked on me again as usual. This time, I screwed up my courage remembering what my dad said and I went after him. He was surprised that I did that, so he stopped. When he stopped, I caught him. I immediately threw him down on the road, got on top of him, ground his head, arms, and legs into the dirt, pounded on him, and made regular mincemeat out of him. When I finally let him up, he was crying and went into his mother's home. About half an hour later, he came outside and was bandaged from one end to the other: both knees, both elbows, across his forehead, across his face, and across his shins. He looked like a walking commercial for Johnson & Johnson. That ended my being bullied.

Chapter 2: Time to Start School

In 1944 at the age of six, it was time for me to go to school. I couldn't attend public school because there were no programs for people with visual limitations. I had to go to a special school. My parents told me about this, but I'm sure I didn't fully understand. On a cloudy September day just after Labor Day, we piled into the family's 1936 Ford Sedan and drove 185 miles to Pittsburgh, PA. When we got there, my mother was crying. She could not get out of the car and come into the school. Dad got the dirty job of taking me in and registering me. This was my first day at the Western Pennsylvania School for Blind Children.

After I was admitted and fully registered, I was taken to a building which was called the Kindergarten Building. I was taken into a dining room and there were several people. Some of them seemed very strange. They were playing in their own way by walking around the dining room with their hands held out in front of them and behaving very strangely. One little boy I saw was very dark in color. I had no idea that everybody in the world was not white.

After about an hour of playing with these strange kids who were yelling and walking around with their hands out in front of them, it was time for dinner. We were ushered to specific chairs seated around the dining room tables. I was placed next to this child who was dark in color. Not knowing why there was somebody of color, I asked the house mother about it. She explained that not everybody in the world is white. The house mother assumed I had a negative reaction, and I was promptly removed from the dining room, taken to the upstairs and a hairbrush was applied to the seat of my pants.

It was only after some discussion with the house mother that administered my first whipping at school realized I was from rural Central Pennsylvania and I had no idea that there were people in the world with dark colored skin. The house mother apologized vociferously to me for assuming I was having a negative reaction to black people. This was my introduction to the Western Pennsylvania School for Blind Children. I spent the next twelve years at the blind school except for Summer Vacations, Thanksgiving, Christmas and Easter.

I would like to pause and make some personal remarks about the subject of race. My story about meeting my first black student, is not intended to offend anybody. It's difficult to say what will and what won't. I should point out that just because I had this initial six-year-old reaction to someone whose skin was a different color than mine, our prejudices were very minimal at blind school. We lived in an institution and were all treated the same. Skin color, religious upbringing, and poverty level did not factor into how you were treated at school. We slept in the same rooms, went to the same classes, ate together and lived together day after day. There were no distinctions made. In fact, in my experience, especially totally blind people, there is no concern or racism towards people of a different color. The hard fact is people with vision problems simply can't see the color of your skin. We have no concept of color. Visually impaired people share the experience of discrimination, not because of race, but because of vision. Therefore, we have something in common with those who experience racial discrimination.

All of my experiences at the School for the Blind could be a book on its own. Enrolling me in the school for the blind was a difficult decision for my parents to make. It was a no-win situation. Half of their community felt they should send me away to this special school. The other half felt that it was a sign of rejection and they should try to get me into the public school or keep me at home and try to educate me the best they could. The community was very divided, and my parents had to listen to everyone's objections. Not many parents would have had the strength to handle this type of controversy with their child. While at school, I learned there were many children rejected by their parents because they were blind. They were placed in foster care, left with grand-parents, or placed in the system some other way. Enrollment at school was 135 when I first started. We lived on a five-acre campus. Many of the students were severely disturbed. Some students lost their sight through bad accidents, such as being stuck in the eye with a golden rod or shot with a

Bibi gun or with a bow and arrow, or in one case; eyes were blown out by a dynamite charge. These were the students I lived, slept, ate, and went to school with for the next twelve years. There was a variety of staff who lived there. Some were college students who used the blind school as a place for room and board and to earn money while they were in school. Some were people who were teachers but could not successfully instruct at the public schools because they were blind.

The day after I entered blind school, we were placed into a small classroom with little desks, typical of any other school. We were going to start learning to read. Reading for me meant you got a book, put it up to your face, and read with your eyes. After all, that's what my parents and younger brother did. At school, I learned it was going to be different for me. A book was placed on the desk in front of me and my hands were placed on it. There were little raised dots in the book which meant absolutely nothing to me. Gradually, the teacher tried to teach me to use my fingers to go over the dots and distinguish them. I immediately picked up the book and put it towards my eyes. The teacher corrected me and said, "No, put the book back down." She repositioned my fingers back on the dots. I didn't understand. It became clear to the teacher that I insisted on using my eyes, because

I had limited sight. She took an apron, placed it around my neck and put it over the book with my hands underneath the apron. I wasn't able to use my eyes and look at the book. This was the beginning of learning Braille.

Through the years, numerous people asked me how long it took for me to learn how to read Braille. The only answer I could give them was by asking, "How long did it take you to learn print?" Braille was my primary source of reading all the way through High School.

Living quarters at school were segregated by gender. There were more boys than girls, but nonetheless, the living quarters were divided accordingly. It was the same in the dining area and in the classroom. Once we reached High School, tables weren't segregated. Laundry was done for us by being placed in assigned laundry boxes. There was a regular routine for changing shirts, slacks, socks, and underwear. The same routine prevailed weekly. Even at six years old, we were expected to wear neck ties and sweaters even during the hottest days of the year. The dress code gradually relaxed as I got older.

One of the things I became very good at while at school was going out to service clubs and demonstrating the use of Braille with a slate and stylus. The school was given money for our presentations. This was one of their major fundraisers. They used their best and brightest students in which I was included.

Blind school was an institutional kind of living with a very set routine that everybody followed. It was almost like being in the military. When I came to school, I was not able to button up my clothes, buckle my own belt, fasten my suspenders and couldn't dress myself. This was frustrating for my mother because she couldn't teach me such skills previously. By the time I came home for my first Thanksgiving vacation, I had learned how to dress myself and perform other basic tasks my mother tried to teach me and couldn't.

School days started by getting out of bed at 6:30 AM. We had 30 minutes to get dressed, ready for breakfast, and seated at the dining room table by 7:00 AM. We sat in the same seats daily. We had 30 minutes to eat. 7:30 AM we were back upstairs in our rooms making beds and taking care of chore assignments until 8:30 am. Next, we went to what was called, "Chapel." It was an assembly all students attended. We sat in the same seats daily Monday through Friday. We were excused from Chapel on Saturdays and Sundays because many of the students went home for the weekend. I was one of the few who remained at the school during most weekends.

One can lose their identity in institutional living. For example, when I first came to school, my parents called me Dick or Dicky. When I arrived at school, I was told there was another boy named Dicky. He was older than I, so the school told me I would be called Richard. From that day on, I was known as Richard at the school until I graduated. At home, my parents still called me Dick or Dicky. I remember an incident from when I was about six or seven years old. My parents sent me a package. The package contained a set of 30 building blocks with pictures of animals on them. I was delighted to receive something from home. When the package was opened, the house parents told me, "Okay. This is not really yours. It has to be shared with all other students." I watched as my building blocks disappeared among the other toys, never to be returned to me again. After that, I told my parents to not send me anymore packages since I couldn't keep them. This was true for all students.

As we moved up through the grades, some of the rules began to change and relax a bit. When I was in sixth or seventh grade, we got a new superintendent; a younger man who had very different ideas about how to run the school. He loosened some of the restrictions. We still had a routine, but it was not as strict and rigid.

When I reached high school, we were a class of ten students. I was one of the two students separated out as a college preparatory student. We studied Latin, English, Algebra, Geometry, and the option to take French if we wished. I refused that. I didn't like French and it wasn't required. You can imagine that a class of only two people for college preparatory was almost like being individually tutored. There were four of us in my Latin class and I remember an incident. One day, we were reading, "Julius Caesar." The three other students in that class did not study and stumbled over the reading which led to the teacher becoming very upset. It came time for me to read and I also stumbled over a few of the words, but it was because some of the Braille dots were worn and rubbed down in my book. This made it difficult to read. The teacher exploded and lost her patience and said to me, "You're getting a failing mark for the day." I slammed my book closed. She told me to open my book and I told her, "No. If I'm getting a failing grade for the day, I intend to earn it." I was taken to the principal's office and I was chastised for my conduct, but the principal told the teacher, "The boy has a point. If you're going to fail him for the day, why should he work anymore."

There was another episode in high school that I remember very well occurring with my English teacher, who actually was one of my favorite teachers. We had four marking periods each year that consisted of nine weeks each. During the end of one of the nine weeks, the teacher explained to us her grading system and what she had changed. She was now grading on a three-score basis; four points was an A, three points a B, two points a C, one point or less was a failure. She gave me a grade of 3.5, halfway between an A and a B. One other student in the class, a girl, was given a grade of 3.7. The teacher gave her an A with outstanding achievement. She asked if there were any questions. I said, "This girl has a 3.7 and I have a 3.5. If she has an A outstanding, I feel that my grade is close enough that it should at least be an A. If on the other hand you take away the outstanding and simply give her the A, I'd be comfortable accepting the B." When the final grades came out, I received an A and June, the girl, received an A with outstanding achievement. In this instance, I think the teacher was very fair.

One of the courses available to me when I reached high school was piano tuning. We would go over to the shop where the pianos were, and our teacher would instruct us on how to do the tuning. I studied piano tuning for four years. By the end of my second year, I was quite comfortable with tuning pianos. I felt the course was necessary for me to take, rather than Industrial Shop. As far as I'm concerned, I had no business messing around with jigsaws and other power tools of that nature. When I was home during vacations, I tuned pianos for money. At my high school graduation, I received my certification from the Piano Tuners and

Technicians Guild to be a certified piano tuner. This skill profited me greatly at various points in my life.

We had visits from time to time from famous celebrities. One celebrity was Helen Keller, who came with her teacher Annie Sullivan. She gave us a little talk and was introduced to many of us. She was quite a hero at that time among blind people. Helen Keller was deaf and blind. Another celebrity that came to visit us my first year in High School was the famous cowboy star Gene Autry. Younger readers may not know anything of him, except that he died just a few years ago at the age of 100. He was also the owner of the Los Angeles Angels baseball team. During the 30's, 40's, and early 50's he made numerous cowboy western movies along with the famous cowboys like Roy Rogers. He gave us a little talk. He was on tour in the Pittsburgh area at that time. At the end of his speech, he wanted to sing us his famous theme song, "Back in The Saddle Again," but he didn't have a guitar. I went up to my room, got under my bed, pulled out my old Craftsman Sears and Roebuck guitar, and brought it down. Mr. Autry played my guitar as he sang his famous theme song. I was a stupid 14-year-old kid at that time and didn't have the sense to have him sign it. Poor me. There were many other famous visitors while I was in school, but these two sticks out in my mind the most.

During my twelve years at school, I was home only for holidays and summer vacation. Home became a problem because I spent most of my time at the school, and that's where all of my friends were. My brother was four years younger and had his own friends. Sometimes I hated coming home for vacations because I missed my friends and the activities, I was accustomed to. Two of the summers that I was in school, I went to a special camp for blind children in Vermont, a beautiful camp called Camp Wapanaki. There was a lake. We had boating, swimming, and other activities. We were there for one full month. Sometimes during the summer when I was older, I went with my brother to my uncle's farm where we made hay and helped thrash wheat and lived the life of farm kids.

Dick at Camp Wapanaki

Many of my classmates lived close enough to the school and could go home for the day or weekend. My home was almost 200 miles away, so I spent most of my time at the school. It caused a great separation from my family. My brother, for example, was educated in a one room schoolhouse until he completed eighth grade. I was educated in very small classes.

I was a city boy, and my parents were country folk. I was frequently teased by other kids when I was home. I was referred to as a city slicker, four eyes, and on one occasion, the blind bat from Pittsburgh. These were not good times for me and explains why I preferred to not be home much. Home to my brothers is not the same as home is to me. It never was and never will be.

The School for the Blind was not strictly a military complex as I have made it sound. We had athletics and other programs besides academics. For example, we had a gymnasium with an indoor track and a brass pole below it. People ran on the track and slid down the brass pole like a fireman. We had parallel bars, a horse, and mats on which we wrestled. We played a version of Dodgeball. The ball had bells in it so that people could hear it coming. We played baseball at the school. We had a small sand field. The ball was sometimes a rolled-up braille magazine and we used a board, which was taken from the chair caning shop, as a bat. If we hit the ball and it landed on the sidewalk, that was a single. If it landed beyond the sidewalk on the grass patch, it was a double. If it landed on the sidewalk beyond the grass patch, that was a triple. If the ball hit the fence beyond the last sidewalk, it was a homer. Totally blind people could hit the ball by virtue of the fact that we rolled it on the ground so they could hear it coming.

They would swing the bat and strike the ball. Sometimes we had a ball with bells on it. The pitcher would actually throw the ball underhanded towards the batter. It was remarkable that totally blind kids could pitch the ball in an area where it could be struck by the hitter. And…totally blind kids could hit the ball. Some of the kids could hit really well because they had excellent hearing.

We had a wrestling team. While I was in high school, the wrestling team started to develop and became a really good squad. I remember one afternoon we wrestled a very highly touted team from the South Western part of Pennsylvania. This team had two or three state champions on it. I remember the first match very well because my best friend, Alden, was the 95-pound weight wrestler from our school. He and his opponent went out on the mat, stood several feet apart face to face, and waited for the ref to blow the whistle for the match to start. Alden was wrestling one of the state champions. The referee blew the whistle, the two headed towards each other, Alden went down, hit the 95-pounder with a double leg tackle, threw him on his back, and pinned him in eight-seconds! The team from the South Western part of the state suddenly realized that these blind guys meant business when they wrestled. We gave them a good match and they did beat us, but we were suddenly a highly respected wrestling team when the match was over. We also wrestled teams from other blind schools. We also had cheer-leaders. There were attempts to play touch or flag football. It was a no passing game because nobody could see to catch the ball. Plenty of people could throw it, but only partially visioned teammates could see to catch the ball.

One of the things I remember early on in blind school was the fact that we had some people who were very ill. One that I remember very clearly from my first year at the school was Jimmy Frowen. Jimmy had a slight depression in his skull which came about as the result of a brain opera-tion to remove a tumor. Jimmy delighted in showing people the dent in his skull where the operation had taken place. He would take a person's hand and place one of their finger's in the dent to show them where the operation was. When I returned from the summer vacation and went into second grade, Jimmy was not there. He died over the summer. His tumor was apparently cancerous. When I came back from my third-grade summer, George Kennedy, who also had a brain tumor died. In fourth grade, when I returned, Wesley Hines had burned to death in a house fire. And at the end of sixth grade, Janet Beard had died causes unknown. When I was in high school, Burt Law, a student who had seizure disorder died. Death was very constant among very young people. I suddenly discovered later on in life that I had a rather callused attitude towards death. I expected it. It was part of life. It happened to anybody and everybody and was no respecter of age, no respecter of health, and no respecter for overall condition. I don't cry when people die. It's just the way it is. That's the way it was all through blind school. We had people who died, usually one or two every year.

It was time for me to graduate from blind school. The amazing thing was when it was time to say goodbye to all whom I've grown to know, all of my childhood friends, it would be the last time I would see any of them ever again. Blind school did not prepare me to live in the outside world. Reality in the outside world was different. People could get in their cars and go and do as they pleased. I never had that experience. I never had the experience of dating through High School as many people have. I was, in my own judgement now, immature, naive, not in any way, shape or form ready for normal sighted world life. If there is one constant lesson to be learned from the blind school experience, it is this; "The world owes you nothing." This was preached to us throughout my 12 years at the school.

On June 10, 1956, I left the Western Pennsylvania School for the Blind forever. I left behind all of my childhood friends. They were like my family. They were like my brothers and sisters, and on the day I left, I would never see them again.

Picture from High School Prom

I came home for the summer not knowing what was going to happen. I planned to make a bunch of money as a piano tuner but didn't know what to do beyond that. I had to learn to live with my brother and parents. My mother wanted to pick up from exactly where she was with me when I was six years old and left for school. I was 18 and developed a fair amount of independence. My mom found it difficult dealing with me. She was not accustomed to dealing with more than one boy at a time; now she had two. She was also pregnant with my youngest brother Bob. She was not in a good mood because of all the stress and strain from pregnancy. In September 1956, I left home again to start at Penn State University.

Dick's High School Senior picture

Chapter 3: Beginning College

In June of 1956, I graduated from the Western Pennsylvania School for Blind Children as valedictorian of my class. To me, it was no great honor because there were only ten people in the class. It's too bad that most of our classes today are so much larger in number because with only ten people in the class, my education was quite good. In fact, only two of us in the class were college preparatory students. Therefore, it was almost like being individually tutored in every subject. I came out of class not knowing what I was going to do, came home at the age of almost eighteen to my parent's little farm in rural Central Pennsylvania with no idea as to what was going to happen in my future. I had learned some skills at the school for the blind, one of them being piano tuning, which in fact, had already netted me a good deal of money since I started doing that when I was about fourteen. And for a while, I thought maybe that was going to be the kind of living I would make.

The summer was hot, and one day in July, two guys in suits came to our house and asked to speak to me. They said they were representatives of the Pennsylvania State Council for the Blind, now part of the Vocational Rehabilitation System. They told me that I had an excellent school record, was valedictorian of my class, and had a very high-grade point average, "Would I like to go to college?" That was a shock. I said yes, I probably would. "You have two choices: You can either go to the University of Pennsylvania, in Philadelphia, or you can go to the Pennsylvania State University in State College, PA." I chose Penn State because it was only 50 miles from home, and I could get home on the weekends. I had spent most of my life not being around my parents and family. I had one younger brother and felt like I needed to spend some time with him and my parents since we didn't really know each other very well. I had been reared quite differently from my brother.

In September, my father took me to the Pennsylvania State University and dropped me at the dormitory where I was supposed to live. Our dormitories then were converted Army Barracks. We had a big furnace at one end of the place that heated the entire barracks. Other than that, we had small rooms; each one with a ceiling light and a light string on it. Penn State even then was a very large campus with well over 20,000 people. I sat in the lobby of the dormitory and I wondered, "What in the name of God am I doing here?" I had no idea how to register for my classes, I had no idea what buildings were where and no idea about anything at all. Across the lobby from me was a payphone. I looked at it, fumbled in my pocket for change, and thought, "For $0.55, I can call home and my Dad will come and get me." I almost made the call, but one of the other guys from the dorm came out and saw me and said, "Don't worry son." He was a Korean War Vet who was there on the GI Bill, "Everything will be okay. My buddies and I will take care of you." And in fact, they did!

They showed me all of the buildings, which I was expected to know, they took me to register for my classes, showed me what buildings my classes would be in, and basically oriented me to the campus and to campus life. I consider myself this day to be very fortunate to have been in a dormitory with so many Korean War Vets, all of whom were very kind to me. Thus, began my college career at Penn State.

Squirrel

One of the guys who lived in the dorm with me and the Korean War vets was a wise guy from Philadelphia. He looked down on people from Central Pennsylvania as many from the city did. He touted himself as a tough Philadelphia street kid. Most people ended up not liking him very well. The older Korean War vets mostly ignored him. At that time at Penn State, if you were a hunting enthusiast, you could actually bring your rifle or shotgun to campus, keep it in your dorm, and go hunting in the surrounding area of the university. Many of the Korean War vets did.

I remember one evening when the Vets came back from hunting and one of them shot a squirrel and gutted it. Our rooms in that dorm were easy to break into. Locks could be picked quite easily. If you remember, those rooms had a ceiling light that was turned off and on with a string that dangled down from the ceiling. The Korean War vets took the gutted squirrel, tied it by the tail on the Philadelphia kid's ceiling light string, locked his door, and left. When he came in later that evening, we were all studying in the dorm. We heard a humungous scream as the kid opened his door, walked in, reached for his light string, and got a fist full of gutted squirrel. He was not such a tough kid from Philadelphia. He didn't stay in the dorm much longer. He requested to be moved to another dorm. I'm not even sure that he ultimately lasted out the first year, but he did get a lesson in humility from the old Korean War vets in my dorm.

John's Snowman

Another fun episode we had in that dorm occurred when John, one of the Korean War vets, was graduating in the wintertime. This was the second year of my tour at Penn State. We wanted to send John on his way remembering us well. One day when he went to lunch, it snowed. We broke into his room and turned off his heat. Two of the guys built a snowman outside the dorm, brought it in, and placed it in the middle of the floor in John's room. They pinned a note to the snowman congratulating him on graduating and hoping he would have something to remember us by. John ultimately went on to Perdue University where he studied graduate work in Engineering. He had written back to some of the guys later on that he remembered quite well the snowman in the middle of his room.

A New Friend

The Korean War veterans weren't my only help during my time at Penn State. One evening as I sat in my dorm room and pondered everything I was going to have to study the first semester. I heard a guitar coming from down the hall. It was kind of sadly out of tune and the guy playing it wasn't making very good chords. I opened my door and followed the sound down the hall. I came to an open room where a young man sat playing his guitar. I knew I reached the correct place. I stepped in, introduced myself and asked him if he would like me to tune the guitar for him. He said, "Yes…I have trouble doing that." I tuned the guitar, and he was quite amazed. He asked,

"How did you do that?" I replied, "I have absolute pitch. Most people don't." We became good friends from that time on. To this day, he now lives with his wife in McEllhatten, PA, near my son and daughter. I see him on occasion. We have remained good friends through all the years and recently, he gave me his Martin guitar, which he can no longer play. He is a journalist and has a son and daughter and grandchildren. We see each other rarely, but it's as though no time has ever passed since we last saw one another.

Gamma Delta

College was interesting for me. I had difficulty studying because I had no idea how to do all of the library work that was required. It was obviously much different for me than high school. We did not have Braille textbooks. There were no tape recorders. My only reprieve was to take classroom notes with my Braille pocket slate and stylus. Fortunately, I found the Delta Gamma Sorority, whose national project is reading to blind students. I was assigned 15 hours of reading per week to cover all of my studies. Every hour, a new reader would come by. We had regular weekly reading schedules. If I was fortunate and everybody showed up, I would actually have the 15 hours a week to study. Most professors would tell you that they wanted you to study at least three hours a week in their class alone. If I followed what was recommended,

I should have had 45 hours of study. I had 15. I did not date. I did not participate in many extra-curricular activities. I felt it necessary to do everything in my power to have a decent grade point average. If I didn't retain a good grade point average, I would have been dismissed from school. Even with those handicaps, I managed to do a better than B average through my studies at Penn State. I graduated in the top 20% of my class. Considering the reading situation, the fact that no tape recorders, no computers, none of the technological aides that people have today existed back then, I consider it a great accomplishment.

The Archer

During my Freshman year, I was required to take some kind of Physical education course. Penn State had developed a series of courses in which they called PhysEd 10, Physical Education for disabilities. My lack of vision qualified me for it. The program included such sports like Bowling, Shuffleboard, Archery, and others that were simple and easy for people to do. It did not specify when you signed up which specific activity you would get.

When I received my registration card for the PhysEd course, they told me I had signed up for Archery and that I was to report to the field where Archery classes were held.

As we gathered together for our first class, I noted that there were all kinds of disabilities there. I was standing next to an individual who was on crutches because he was born without legs. He was given a bow and arrow; it became clear that this was not going to be a good course for him. Every time he chose to pull back the bow and let the arrow fly, he lost his balance and fell. The arrow usually went sailing off into the air somewhere. Standing next to him, I felt rather threatened. The arrow could have come and struck me during its journey back to the ground. I wouldn't have been able to get out of the way in time since I couldn't see it coming. It would have been too late for me.

The coach came down the line and asked each person their disability. When he came to the guy with no legs, he could easily see what his disability was and said, "I don't think Archery is a good idea for you given you can't maintain your balance as you pull back on the bow." When he came to me, he looked at me and said, "You look kind of normal. What is your disability?" I told him that I had very limited vision. He put his hands over his face and said, "How do we deal with this?" I replied by saying, "Look...I can't see the target out there, but if we pace it off, I will have some idea of distance." He did as I suggested. We paced it off so that I knew what the distance was, and I knew the general vicinity of the hay bales with the targets on them.

Archery is a matter of form. If you do the correct form, and do the same thing every time, your arrow will go where it is aimed. I had to concentrate quite severely on having the proper form and gauging the proper distance. The Archery course lasted eight weeks and there was a tournament the last day. After all of the scores were taken, yes folks; I won the tournament. The coach just couldn't wrap his mind around it, especially considering I was the only one in the tournament with limited vision.

We got no award for winning the tournament, but I got a good story out of it and everybody laughed their sides sore when I told my dorm mates what happened. I received an A for that class. Archery became a kind of hobby for me and I did end up buying my own bow and arrow. I set up hay bales and targets at home. I continued to practice Archery for quite some time. I got very good at it.

Marcus

While I was at Penn State for four years, I met some rather interesting characters. One of my favorites was Marcus Ingram. Marcus was a six-foot tall Black man from North Carolina. He was a graduate student of economics and was totally blind. He had graduated from an all-Black college in Durham, where he was from. He was hoping to become an Economics Professor at some point in his life, preferably at a black school. Marcus had a great sense of humor and a big smile. One of his favorite avocations was playing Bridge. Since Marcus also had readers from the Delta Gamma Sorority, we often saw each other at the girl's dorm where we went to study. When Marcus realized I might be interested in learning how to play Bridge, he proceeded to show me. As time went on, we taught all of our readers to play Bridge so that on days when studies were rather infrequent, we could play with two of our readers. Marcus and I played Duplicate Bridge. In fact, when we decided to partner up and play duplicates, we stayed up all night one night and applied Braille to 30 decks of cards so that we could play. We did very well. Every week at the tournament, we always finished at either first or second. We were thought of as the marvels of the whole bridge set.

Marcus often spoke about the situations in the South, which at that time, segregation was at full bloom. Marcus had said to me at one time that he would have liked to have taken me home with him to visit his family, but he knew that it would never work. He said it would be too dangerous for me and also for his family if a white person came to visit in their community. I did, however, take Marcus home with me one weekend to visit my family, who were warmly accepting even though my parents were not familiar with black people. They showed Marcus a good time. One of his hobbies was photography even though he was totally blind from birth. He had a camera and took pictures of my young brother at that time. Marcus also met my horses.

He was a remarkable young man who was very intelligent. Everybody liked Marcus; white, black, whatever. It made no difference. It reminds me of comments I previously made about race while in blind school; racial prejudice had no place in blind schools. We were all treated the same and in speaking with other blind and partially sighted friends, I find that their blind school experiences were exactly the same as mine. There was no room for, no tolerance of, and no expectation of any kind of racial prejudices. Besides, those of us who are blind or partially sighted had to deal with our own prejudices.

Marcus graduated sometime after I did. One summer after I finished at Penn State, Marcus and two of his friends came to visit me at my home for an afternoon. That was the last time I ever saw Marcus. The last I heard anything about him, he was teaching at an all-black school in Alabama. I don't know whether Marcus is still alive or not but will say for certain that he was of one the most unforgettable characters I ever met.

We Hunt No More...

During my first semester in college, tragedy struck our family. On December 15, 1956, my father had gone hunting with a group of his relatives. It was the last day of deer season. It was raining, foggy, cold and wet. There were eight hunters in the group. My father had an artificial leg and had difficulty walking in the woods. He was positioned to move along a road to make travel easy for him. In hunting deer in Pennsylvania, the hunters if in a group usually line up and drive through an area where deer might be located. Each hunter shouts out so that everybody knows where everybody is. As they were driving through deer, my father suddenly saw a deer come out in front of him and to the right. It was a buck and was legitimate prey. He hulled up and fired at the deer. The result was that he heard a loud human groan. He suddenly knew that his bullet had probably struck a human being.

He began to work his way in the direction of where he heard the human groaning come from. As he did, he took a knife and marked the trees along his route. He finally came to the person who had yelled. The person was down on the ground with a bullet in his leg, bleeding profusely. The other hunters eventually gathered around and formed a tourniquet. They also made a litter out of their belts and a couple of saplings. They ran to the car with the individual who had been shot. They placed him in the car with a couple of people to hold him in the back seat while they drove 20 miles to the nearest hospital.

They arrived at the emergency room where the individual died almost immediately. The bullet from my father's gun, which was a Marlin 35 rifle, had struck him in the upper leg. It had blown the entire bone out of the leg. The bullet went in like a Bibi and came out like a basketball. It severed the femoral artery causing the individual to bleed to death. The even greater tragedy was the individual was my dad's nephew. He was 27, married, and had two small girls ages three and four. Part of the hunting group that had been with dad included the boy's father.

For several days, my dad sat around drinking coffee going over and over the incident. No charges were filed since it was very clear that he had shot at the deer, missed the deer, and in a one in a million chance, struck the leg of his nephew. Of course, this influenced my adjustment at school. It was horribly difficult seeing my dad suffer the way he did. At one point, he finally said to my mother and me that he had a dream. He saw his nephew in the dream. He was all dressed in white. The nephew told him that he forgave him for what happened, that it was not his fault, and that it could not have been helped. Dad seemed to have finally settled the matter in his mind, but he was never the same after that.

My dad and my brother Ken were avid hunters, going for small game and deer. They never went out again. Ken witnessed the accident. He was one of the people who held my dad's nephew down in the back seat on the way to the hospital as he slowly bled to death. To this day, Ken does not hunt. My youngest brother Bob does not hunt either. Most people in our family have given up small game and deer hunting. My dad did try to go hunting a year or two after the accident, but he stated that he just couldn't do it. All he could do is see danger and he got rid of his guns.

Dick's Senior Year at Penn State

Chapter 4: My Brothers

Kenny

I had come home from blind school after graduating in June 1956 and started college at Penn State in September of that same year. Fortunately, Penn State was located only around 50 miles from home. This allowed me the opportunity to come home over weekends when there were no classes. I managed to get to know my family, especially my younger brother Ken. I discovered quickly that I didn't know his friends and had none of my own in the Valley where my parents lived. My brother made every effort to try to include me in some of his activities. His friends were all four to five years younger than I and we had very little in common.

We purchased a car together and used it for Ken's paper route. He made a fair amount of money each week. Sometimes on the weekends I would ride with him on his route. It covered 50 miles over a rural area where we delivered the Philadelphia Inquirer, the Philadelphia Bulletin, and the Williamsport Grit, also known as the Pennsylvania Liar. At each stop where we delivered a paper, we would collect money and usually ended up with a large bag of change. My brother also had a local paper route delivering the local Lock Haven paper the Express. That route covered some 25 to 30 miles. Obviously, he put a good number of miles on the car.

In 1960, we decided that between us we had enough money to purchase a new car. We went to several car dealers and checked out some vehicles. Ultimately, we ended up buying a 1960 Ford Falcon. It was the first year of that model. That same year, Chevrolet also produced the Corvair. Of course, the big question was, "Which car was faster…the Falcon or the Corvair?" One of my brother's friends that lived just down the road from us had purchased a Corvair. It was decided that my brother and his friend would get together and race their cars down the back road of the Valley six miles to the nearest town.

I rode in the car with my brother and two of his friends. The Corvair driver had three people in his car. We lined up and at a given signal, we took off. The Falcon bounced over some dips and hills on the road. One occasion, we actually went airborne and landed on all four wheels that threw sparks as we landed. When the six-mile race was over, the Falcon had defeated the Corvair by a substantial margin.

My brother and I along with two other people near our ages built a shanty, a small cabin up in the woods where we camped out periodically. We had a good time there. We often went fishing at the stream nearby and fried fish for breakfast. We also put eggs in a jar and kept them in the stream overnight so that they stayed cold and would also cook them for breakfast in the mornings. My dad came along to help us build the cabin since he knew more about carpentry than we did. The other boys basically built the cabin as I sat and watched or carried boards and nails to them as they were needed. In this regard my brother and I did have some peers in common and we had some shared experiences. In 1961, we traded in our 1960 Falcon and bought another Falcon. During that year, my brother ended up getting a job with the Justice Department in Washington, DC and left home.

The Inauguration of JFK

In January 1961, after graduating college and I was still waiting around to find a job. My parents and I drove to Washington, DC to John F. Kennedy's inauguration. I remember the drive very well because as we arrived at the Baltimore-Washington Expressway, it began to snow. We were tied up in traffic behind several cars with no one getting anywhere. In the South, people don't know how to drive in the snow.

After eight hours of stop and go traffic through the snow, working our way around abandoned cars, which had run out of gas or batteries that died, even just parked and left on the roadway, we made it into Washington, D.C... We contacted my brother, who got us tickets to the inauguration since he worked in the Justice Department. He managed to come up to where we were waiting and guided us through the rest of the city to where we were staying. Mom and Dad stayed in a hotel room. I stayed with my brother and his roommates in their apartment.

The next day, we went to the Kennedy Inauguration and heard the famous speech. Every time I hear about John F. Kennedy and his inaugural speech that included the famous quote, "Ask not what your country can do for you. Ask what you can do for your country," I'm reminded of the amazing fact that I was there in person to see and hear it.

Later, dad, mom and I stood with my brother and a few of his friends on the corner of Constitution Avenue and watched the inaugural parade. It was cold. There were at least ten inches of snow on the ground. The cars were cleaned up from being abandoned all over town. It was so cold, that my brother and I on two or three occasions during the parade, walked into the Archives Building in order to get warm. My dad, who loved parades, never once left the street corner.

Once again, I was somewhat by myself, except for my four-year-old brother Bob. He was born just two months after my dad's hunting accident. In fact, his birth had helped my dad get through that very difficult time. Ken only stayed at his job in Washington, DC until sometime in 1962. He decided to come back home because he had a girl in the area, and he wanted to marry her. He took a job with a local chemical plant where he worked until he retired.

Ken with his older brother Dick

Bob

As my brother Ken married and left home, I was left to work with my youngest brother who was born February 1957. As he grew older, I began to do more things with him. I showed him how to ride horse back. We played our version of ball. I couldn't hit a baseball, but I could show him somewhat how to do that. I could play catch with him if we weren't standing too far apart. I got him his first bicycle and showed him how to ride it.

In many respects, I was more like a father to him than a brother. After all, my dad was an amputee and not athletic. I was more athletic but had limited eyesight, so I had to stay within my limits. I got to show my little brother how to do things that boys and their fathers do. My dad was older and not able to do these things in an energetic way. As my youngest brother started getting older, he became interested in mechanics. As he grew up, he decided to become a vehicle mechanic and went to school for training in that regard.

Today, he owns a very large towing business that employs about 20 to 25 people. He has a number of tractor trailer wreckers and cleans up accidents along Interstate 80 in the central part of Pennsylvania. He is successful and has done very well for himself. I will say as a little boy, no one would have ever expected that he would do as well as he has done.

Bob tried to do things with our father. I remember one episode when dad was painting our kitchen. Dad was trying to reach up high to do some painting. He would step up on a ladder with a paint roller then step back down to fill the roller in the pan. Dad gave Bob a brush to help paint and gave him a little section of the wall to do down low. As dad would step up and down off the step stool, Bob decided to do the same thing. He would step up on the stool and paint. One of the times Bob stepped down and put his foot in the paint pan. My dad immediately began to yell at him and became upset with him. Bob replied, "Now dad, after all…I am just a child."

The Bressler Boys with their parents

Chapter 5: It All Started with a One-Eyed Horse

I was in my third year of college. All the other guys my age in the Valley where my parents lived had cars, girlfriends, and things to do. I had some money of my own I earned by selling magazines, Christmas cards and other items. I also at the age of 21 received what was then called Blind Pension. Today it's called SSI. I told my father I wanted to get a horse. If I couldn't have a car, I could at least have a horse. My mother threw a fit. She swore I'd get killed having a horse. She swore I wouldn't be able to handle it. She swore that it was a bad idea, a bad investment of my money. My father in his wisdom said, "He has his own money. He's entitled to do with it as he wants. We have the farm here. He can have a horse. There's plenty of pasture, there's water, there's a barn; he can certainly have a horse." My father continued with a but and said, "You don't know anything about horses, and I know very little. So, when you go to buy a horse, I'm going with you." Fair enough. I needed a ride anyway.

We went to a farm about 15 miles away near a town called Jersey Shore and met with a horse trader who had several horses for sale. The horse that I finally bought was Old Marge. Marge was a Paint; brown and white. She looked a lot like the Lone Ranger's horse Scout from the old TV show, but Marge had a double arrowhead brand on her right leg, which also had a tremendous scar having been caught in barbed wire. I was told that she was originally a cow pony from Oklahoma. Whether that's true or not, to this day I don't know. She had one eye as a result of an encounter with barbed wire. This horse and I had one good eye between us and it was hers. We came home. I got a saddle and bridal with her. A couple of guys from the riding club in the Valley came by and taught me how to saddle and bridal this horse. I learned some things the hard way. For example, did you know that horses will often hold their breath when you go to saddle them so that you think the saddle is tight. Once you're cinched up, they let their breath out, thus loosening it up so that when you put your foot in the stirrup to mount the saddle, you usually end up on the ground with the saddle sliding down on top of you. I learned that lesson from Old Marge.

When riding Old Marge, she would frequently cross her front feet, which was a most uncomfortable walk. She would take me under tree branches trying to brush me off. On a couple of occasions, we were walking along, and she would lie down as if she were going to roll, making it necessary for me to get off of the saddle to prevent myself from being rolled on. All in all, Old Marge taught me how to ride, and I ended up teaching her who was boss.

I paid $150.00 for her; a horse that would otherwise have most likely not been purchased, but God was with me. Old Marge, unknown to the person I bought her from, was pregnant. 11 months after I bought her, my last day of college finals, Old Marge gave birth to a colt. The colt was a little chestnut mare, and I named her Jewel because she had a diamond on her forehead. Jewel and I were great pals along with Old Marge. It was my brother Bob, then aged 6 or so, that learned how to ride the colt and helped me break her. I also bought a sulky, a two wheeled pony cart, and taught Jewel to harness and pull the sulky. I had a rubber-tired buggy, a spring wagon with a covered top and a fringe, and a sleigh with beautiful red velvet cushions. All in all, during the time of my career with horses, I had six different ones. I had some great adventures with them. I rode with the local riding club on several outings, had a great time, and finally felt like I belonged to something in the Valley.

Bob helping Dick with Old Marge

Bob helping Dick with Jewel

I later sold my old one-eyed horse since she wasn't able to do much anymore and purchased other horses more suited for riding. I kept her until I went to Graduate School. I had to sell Jewel because there was nobody around to take care of her. My youngest brother was too small to assume that responsibility. My second year at grad school, I missed the horses and decided to buy a one-year-old Arabian stallion colt named Duke. Duke and I had a rather bad accident that ended my horse-riding career.

Duke was a beautiful horse with a reddish color and a white blazed face. I trained Duke right from the very beginning. I put a saddle on him and again used my youngest brother to ride him as I lead him around. I taught him the bit and bridal. He was a gentle horse, not like most stallions. By the time Duke was two years old, he was ridable. In the summer of 1965 after my first year of Graduate school, I was out riding with Duke when two women riding a motorcycle came up from behind me. They were yelling and screaming. They were heading for the construction that was going on for Interstate 80 at that time near my parent's house. Duke got scared and decided to run. I thought that if all he was going to do was run, that was no problem. But when his feet went out from under him and he went down, that was a problem. I managed to swing my feet out from the stirrups and go over to the side as a partial dismount. I didn't quite make it off of the horse when he finally hit the ground. My legs were underneath him. We slid down the macadam road for several feet until stopped. Duke had a major gash on his hip. Both of my knees were torn to the bone. I couldn't get up and walk, but I held on to the saddle horn and the bridal so that when Duke got to his feet, he pulled me up to mine. The problem was he wanted to walk away, and I couldn't walk with him. I wrapped the bridal around the saddle horn and let go of Duke. I had to sit down on the road since I wasn't able to stay on my feet. Now, you've seen the old Western movies and they always manage to say or imply that when you are disabled from your horse, your horse is supposed to go home and get help. Duke decided to walk along the side of the road and began grazing. He made no effort to go home, which was about a mile away.

I finally picked up a few stones from the road and threw them at him. I crawled to the side of the road since I clearly didn't want to get hit by a car. Duke finally ambled down the road towards home, but he took his good old time. Finally, my neighbor came along in her car and stopped. She saw that I was pretty bloody and that I wasn't able to get up or do anything. She helped get me in her car and back to my house we went. I showed my injuries to my mother and she said, "I can't fix this. We have to go to the emergency room." At that time, I had a cousin that was an emergency room nurse, and I was her first patient that day, just after 3:00 pm. Both knees were stitched together by a young dermatologist that just joined the staff. He was a kind man and was an Air Force doctor that just served his term. He was looking to begin some kind of an independent practice. He asked me what I did, and I told him how I was a Graduate student and was expected to go back that coming fall. I told him that I had no money as a student. For seeing me in the hospital, giving me a pair of crutches and stitching up both knees, he charged me $20.00.

For the next several weeks I could not bend my knees. They were stitched up to the point that I had to keep my legs straight. This presented quite a problem when going to the bathroom, as you could imagine. We figured it out and made it work. I looked like a walking commercial for Johnson & Johnson as I was bandaged all over, having cuts and scrapes not only on both knees, but both elbows, both wrists, and several other places. After a few weeks, I decided I was not going to let Duke to the care of my 7-year-old brother as I went back to Graduate school in Pittsburgh. I sold Duke and got more money for him that what I originally paid for. That was the end of the horse business for me. I have not ridden a horse since and probably never will.

Chapter 6: Almost A Veteran

It was the mid-1960's and the nation had been given the order of a draft for military purposes, largely because of the Vietnam War. On a regular basis, people were being called to their draft boards for examination and possible induction into the armed services. To my surprise, I received a notice in the mail from my local draft board to appear to be considered for the draft. This was kind of strange because being a person of low vision, I should have been automatically excluded to go for the exam however, that wasn't the case. My dad took me the twenty miles over to Lock Haven, the county seat, where the draft board was located.

When I got there at 5:30 in the morning, there were several other guys who had also been summoned for their draft examination. A lady on the steps of the draft board office called out, "Bressler?" I answered her and she said, "You're in charge of the group." And she handed me a whole series of papers, none of which I could read. A friend of mine who was also summoned and stood next to me in the group said, "Don't worry. I'll help you out with this."

We boarded a bus and were taken to Wilkes Barre, PA, where the draft induction center was. We got inside the building and were ushered into a room which had several little desks. It reminded me of a first-grade classroom. These were uncomfortable little fellas considering most of us were full-grown and had to squeeze ourselves into the childish desks they had there. On top of the desks was a paper, which we were told over the PA system, was a copy of the Armed Forces Qualification Test, also known as the AFQT. This was basically an IQ test.

The sergeant who was giving instructions over the PA system gave us several sample questions and told us how to answer them. They were all multiple choice. When we received the first question, he read off the multiple choices and then he said, "Your correct answer should be D. Take your pencil and mark in the block D." Not being able to read the exam, I didn't know where block D was, so I left my pencil lay on the desk. This sergeant came around, picked up my pencil, shoved it in my hand and marked the block D. He said, "This is the way you do it son, it's just very simple.' I started to tell him, "No." This wasn't simple for me because I couldn't read it. He simply ignored me and passed on. Second question. Your answer is to be C. Take your pencil and mark in the block C. Again, I left my pencil lay on the desk because I didn't know where the block C was. Sergeant came by again and said, "It's just this simple sir. Now come on. Pick up your pencil and let's mark in block C." I said, "But sergeant, you don't understand, I…" The sergeant sternly replied, "JUST MARK IN BLOCK C!" He cut me off. The third question came around and I did the same thing. The sergeant got more impatient and told me to mark in the correct block, which again, I did not do because I didn't know where it was.

Finally, a young lieutenant came out and said to me, "What seems to be the problem here?" I explained to the young lieutenant that I couldn't do the exam because I couldn't read it. I did not have the ability to read the exam due to my low vision. He asked me quickly, "Why are you here?" I explained to him that my draft board sent me here. He said, "Hold on a minute." He came back a bit later and said, "We're going to give you the eye test." He marched me to a small hallway. At the far end of the hallway was a large screen. To my left was a series of pads with colors on them. The examiner asked me to recite the colors. I was able to see them, so I recited the colors. He heaved a big sigh and said, "Tell me what is on that big screen down at the end of the hall." I said to him, "I don't even have to look at it. I can tell you it's a big E." He again heaved a big sigh and said, "Take off your glasses." I took them off and he said, "Walk down to that screen until you can read the letter E."

I walked down to the screen and was about three feet from it and said, "Oh yes…that's a letter E." I was taken back to my seat and told after the young lieutenant talked to me for a while that I should wait there for the entire day to pass.

They gave us a boxed lunch. I waited for the entire day to pass while all of the other guys were examined for the draft. Late in the afternoon after everyone was examined, we were called up to the front of the room one at a time and given the results of our examination. When my name was called, I got up, and with some help from my buddy, I walked up to the front of the room where sat this little soldier with thick glasses and a dark head of hair. He had a speech impediment. He said to me with a heavy lisp, "Mr. Bressler, you are a permanent physical reject and unaccept-able for the draft." I thanked him and went back to my seat. I waited until all was finished.

Those who were rejected were sent back home on a bus. We were given paperwork to stop at restaurant in a nearby town where would we be fed at the Army's expense. This proved to be a troublesome thing because nobody believed the Army would feed a whole bunch of guys like that late at night. We had a difficult time convincing the restaurant people. I was able to convince them, and we did get some-thing to eat. We went home and I was taken back to my house by my Dad, whom I called while on our way back to Lock Haven.

Three days later, I got another notice from the draft board that I was to report for examination. I called them up and said I would not be reporting. I was told I could go to jail. I said, "Fine. I have already been rejected. I am 4 F. I am not going through this process again. If you want to take me to jail, I live twenty miles away from you. Come and get me." Of course, they didn't, and nothing ever happened.

Chapter 7: Work

I graduated in 1960, when the world was told if you had an education, you could do anything. I found out that may be true for some sighted people, but it was not true for blind and low vision people. I spent the next nine months looking for work and trying to find a job. I took Civil service exams or tried to. That was impossible because there were no provisions for people with low vision or inability to read. Finally, near the end of my rope, wondering what was going to happen, and listening to my parents talk about the possibility that, "We have one boy who will probably live with us the rest of his life," I found myself looking at a job ad for a school psychiatric social worker.

My uncle was a member of the school board, so I talked to him about the position. He said that I needed to speak to the county judge because he was quite instrumental in securing someone for the job. My dad and I drove 20 miles to the Lock Haven courthouse, walked in and up to the second floor, and asked to see the judge. The judge was standing in the court room watching the painters who were re doing the court room. I introduced myself to him and said that

I came to inquire about the school psychiatric social work position. After giving him my resume, he said," I'm afraid you don't qualify. This requires a master's degree and you only have a BA." In frustration, I said to him, "It's getting difficult for me. The taxpayers paid my way through school and now nobody wants to hire me." This was about 10:30 in the morning.

The judge leaned back from his desk and said to me, "Can you come back at 1:00 PM?" I looked at my dad, he nodded, I said yes. Dad and I browsed around town, got some lunch. We returned at 1:00pm to the courthouse to the judge's chambers. The judge said to me, "We need somebody to supervise juvenile probationers in this county. We are sending too many of them to reform schools because we don't have anyone in the community to watch over them. It's costing us a great deal of money. I cannot give you a job technically and pay you, but if you would be willing, I can pay you some expenses for nine months till the end of the year. If you can prove that you can work with these juveniles, keep the crime rate down, cut the expenses for institutional care, then we may be able to justify a salary for you to have the job." I looked at my dad and asked him, "What do you think?" My dad did his usual wise thing and said, "It's up to you son." I told the judge I'd like to give it a try. For the next nine months, I worked basically for nothing.

I had to pay $0.50 a day to go back and forth to work and also joined a driving pool. At the end of nine months, we cut in half the number of people that were in institutions and a salary was justified. Plus, at that time, the state mandated that the county had to pay me a salary.

We did some interesting things in the juvenile court system. I remember the first day I went to work. At 9:00 AM in the morning, we had a juvenile court hearing. Three boys were sentenced to reform school in Western Pennsylvania. The boys were wearing handcuffs and in the back seat of the car. The chief probation officer and I drove them out and admitted them to the school. We drive back. Stopped for dinner at a restaurant. I got sick and "lost my dinner." I took the next three days off and did not go in until I recovered. When I went back in to work, the judge looked at me and said, "I guess you had a pretty rough first day."

I began to pick up on my duties. It took me a few weeks of interviewing juveniles to understand why these kids were getting into trouble. First, I realized most of them couldn't read. They were doing poorly in school, had very little support at home, no type of tutorial help, and no emotional support. I finally designed a program in which I went to the judge and asked him if I could use the law library for an hour and a half after school. The judge agreed and we called the juveniles in who were under my care. I asked them to bring in their homework and meet after school at the law library by a specified time. I made it a condition of their probation.

There were 20 to 25 kids. We all sat down, and I began to help them with their homework. At first, they complained until I pointed out to them if they got to work and did their assignments, they would be released quickly; or they could whine and complain, waste time meaning they would have to be there longer than what was really needed. They soon got the message and began to buckle down and do their homework. Within one marking period, their grades improved drastically. They began to listen to what I told them they needed to do and stay out of trouble. Furthermore, their parents were much happier with them, especially since they were doing better in school.

Another program I established dealt with the fact that most adolescent boys and girls don't like rules. They didn't understand the point of rules. They were restrictive, limiting, and not to their advantage. Understanding this, I went to the local YMCA directly across the street from the courthouse. I spoke with the director there and we set up a time the kids could play basketball. We played basketball without rules. No teams were set up, people just went out and shot baskets, and interfered with each other any way they felt like doing. Of course, they would complain. I reminded them there were no rules. If you shot and made a basket, it really didn't matter since we didn't keep score. No rules. The kids continued for about 20 minutes of playing without rules. You could imagine the obvious; it was chaotic, nobody could organize anything, and nobody knew what was going on. We switched up the game. We divided up into teams and played for another 20 minutes this time with rules.

After we were done playing, we went back to the courthouse and discussed the importance of rules. We pointed out that rules defined the game and the game's limits. We pointed out that rules are for your guidance. Rules make it easier for you to get along with other people and understand expectations. Pretty soon, I wasn't hearing anymore complaints about rules.

The assassination of JFK

Throughout the course of my life, I have lived through some rather major historical events. One occurred on November 22, 1963. I was working in the Clinton County Probation Department in the courthouse. I just came back from an early lunch and we just began a meeting with several social agency representatives. We were going to discuss the possibility of establishing a private independent counseling service in the area. I stepped out for a bathroom break and as I walked through the office, the radio was turned on, and Walter Cronkite, the famous newscaster of CBS was discussing the occurrence that was so important that day.

President Kennedy, along with his wife and entourage, had made a trip to Dallas. While driving down the street in the motorcade, he was shot from the second floor of the now famous Book Depository. As I was walking through the office, I was listening to the radio. It was nearly 1:00 PM and Walter Cronkite was announcing to the world that the President was assassinated. I walked back into the law library where our meeting was being held and told the social agency people that the President had been assassinated. The meeting ended immediately. There were several reactions about the event. Some people concluded it had to do with the moral breakdown of the country. Others decided that it had to do with political upheaval. It was a shocking experience and normal daily routine activities came to a screeching halt. We ended up going home trying to figure out what was coming next as Vice President Lyndon B. Johnson was sworn in to replace John F. Kennedy as President of the United States.

The Good and the Bad of Juvenile Probation

There were many sad cases I had assigned to me. One of my saddest was a boy whose father was involved with the local volunteer fire company. The boy, in order to impress his father, thought it would be a good idea to set a fire and then heroically helped his father put it out. He was apprehended by the fire marshal, brought in and placed on probation under my supervision. The parents were devastated. They tried to teach their son the differences between what was right and what was wrong. They had no idea he was going to do something like this. The parents made restitution for the fire and ultimately took up better supervision of their son.

I had another juvenile that needed foster care since he couldn't remain at home. In a rather unusual move, I suggested the parents of the fire setter as potential foster parents for this young man who was a thief. The court bought it and agreed with my idea. It went very well. The thief stayed with them until he graduated high school. He ultimately went on his own and as an adult, did quite well for himself. This was a great boost to the family of the fire setter. It helped reduce their shame and sense of failure regarding their own child. Their son ultimately became part of the volunteer fire company where his father worked and to this day, many years later, still operates as a volunteer fireman in his home community.

There were many stories in probation that I could tell however, too numerous for this chapter. It was an exciting life, but it was before the issues we have today. What we learned was that sending kids to reform schools often resulted in their learning more sophisticated ways to be criminal. Keeping them in the community and trying to help them live better lives seemed to be the best way in most instances I experienced. I'm happy to say that many of the clients I served in probation grew up to become productive adults; a fact for which I can't and don't take a great deal of credit, but am nonetheless, very proud. I worked in that position for three and a half years, until I finally decided I needed to know more and attended Graduate School in Pittsburgh.

Even the Blind Can Teach

For a few years, my profession led me to the world of academia and taught at Lock Haven University. Within the first three years of my teaching career there, I taught 12 different courses. Somewhere in the midst of my third year, I was teaching a Sociology course. My style of teaching was to walk around the room, lecture, and watch students take notes. I would walk past their desks to establish closeness with them. I did this during examinations too, which cautioned them to be careful about looking at other people's books or cheat in some way. In this particular class, I had one student who was constantly reading a newspaper. He would come to class and was always reading the newspaper, even during my lectures. Whether he thought I didn't see him or not, I don't know, but it was obvious. Finally, in my travels around the classroom, I walked around, kept on lecturing, and when I came close to him, I pulled out my cigarette lighter and set the newspaper on fire. The kid didn't know what to do. He looked at me and said, "What should I do?" I looked at him and said, "Put it out!"

Teaching at Lock Haven University during the mid to late 60s and early 70s was quite an experience. It was a time of great unrest in the country largely because of opposition to the Vietnam War. Many young people either entered college or went to work in defense plants. They did whatever they could to avoid the draft. I encountered many students who were in college to protect themselves from the draft. I remember one incident while teaching a summer course. A young student came to me and said he was from the Mid-West and needed a particular grade to stay in school. He was not doing well overall. I looked at my grade book and attendance sheet. Back then, we took attendance and were able to penalize students who skipped too many classes. He was one of those students who didn't have a passing grade at the time of finals. I so informed him. He began to plea with me to get a passing grade. Finally, he said to me, "If you don't give me a passing grade, you're as good as sending me to Vietnam." I said to him, "Don't you mean if you don't earn a passing a grade?" I pointed out to him that students always have a habit of saying, "I got an A. You gave me an F." I told him it didn't work both ways. He was responsible for his grade and I was sorry if he ended up going to Vietnam. There was at least one other student who needed a passing grade and didn't have it. She came into my office and said to me, "I need a C in your course." I told her my grade book said she didn't have one. She leaned over wearing a very low-cut dress and said, "I would do anything to get a C." My answer to her was, "There wasn't anything you can do to get a C." This was the kind of situation that one often ran into teaching; students expecting some kind of last-minute reprieve.

One of my favorite stories is the day that I gave a final in a sociology class. The final was an essay question. I assigned the question and they had two hours to answer it. Thirty seconds into the test, a young student came up with a small piece of paper and handed it to me. Written on it was, "Only God knows the answer." I took a pencil and in very large print, which is how I could write, wrote, "God gets an A. You get an F." I handed the paper back to the student, he looked at what I wrote, and he then asked, "Can I do this over again?" I advised him, "I don't really have to do that, but since you realize that you've been kind of an idiot and that there is an hour and 58 minutes left in this exam, you may best get back to your seat and start working on it seriously."

As a," Handicapped" employee, I, like so many others in my situation, have an attitude that I must work much harder than the non-handicapped employee in order to prove my worth. I therefore don't have a great deal of tolerance for people that don't want to work very hard and want to slide through on a minimal effort or dishonest way. I encountered one of those types of students during a summer course. She had come there to earn her public-school teaching certificate, which is required in Pennsylvania. She earned all her courses but one. My class was the last one she needed. I assigned an essay final and when I received her essay back, I looked at it and thought, "This is not this student's writing." I took my work study student that I used as a reader and researcher and went to the library. We pondered through several encyclopedias. I came to the Encyclopedia Britannica and found the article she plagiarized word for word. Of course, I assigned her a failing grade. She protested and came in wanting to know why she got an F. I took the encyclopedia with the article my reader had marked and placed her paper next to it. She threatened to go to the administration. I told her, "We'll go to the administration. I'll take the encyclopedia and your paper along and I think that will settle the matter." She began to cry saying she needed this course to obtain her certification and that if she did not get it, she wouldn't be allowed more time and would probably lose her job. I told her that given the way she behaved as a student; I had some serious question of whether she ought to be a teacher at all. I assume she did lose her job. I never did hear otherwise. I felt she was a student that got what she deserved.

I can think of many other stories, too numerous to mention all of them in this letter but believe these few examples give you some idea of how it was teaching in the 60s and early 70s. By 1971, we had several more staff members than were there when I began. Even though I spent three years teaching 12 different courses, was promoted to Assistant Professor and tenured in the minimum time period, other professionals came and had degrees beyond mine. As the faculty became unionized, I was being criticized for teaching outside my actual field of expertise. I had nothing to do with that and I quickly prompted my critics by saying, "If you have a problem with that, go talk to the department chairman." I got bored in the fourth-year teaching because I was instructing the same course, Beginning Sociology. Before going to the college, I was accustomed to a 40-hour work week, sometimes with overtime doing emergency service. I felt the college professors had easy jobs, yet many of them complained and whined constantly. I felt I had enough of it and didn't really like the college classroom. I much preferred to be out in the field. When the opportunity arose, I left the university and went into mental health/mental retardation services.

Letters to my children

Chapter 8: Mental Health

The first experience with mental health, of course, was with a local counseling agency of which I became the director. During that time, we were under contract but were told that, within a short period of time, the agency contract would be terminated, and the contract would be made with a hospital needing a satellite unit to cover both counties. This transition happened in 1975 and I went from being the director of a small local counseling service to becoming the director of a two-county mental health unit. I managed to ask the hospital to preserve the counseling agency, which I was leading, and to use that agency and staff as the satellite unit, which they needed, for our local county. Fortunately, they agreed to do so, and I was able to preserve the jobs of the people that worked faithfully with me during the 1971-1975 period.

In 1975, I took the director shift of the overall mental health unit. This was the place in which I saw clients who were much more sophisticated than in the previous counseling service. We saw many people who were drug and alcohol related. We saw many people who were psychotic. We saw people who were released from the state hospitals, had no family and no support system, who were to live in the community, and we were to supervise their medications and other treatment. This was a time when we had all kinds of clients, usually people that nobody else wanted to see and people who were unable to pay any great amount of money for their services.

During the course of my stay in the mental health agencies, I had three clients who ultimately committed suicide. There was nothing I could do about any of them. One was an individual who was addicted to a particular narcotic. The supply ran out, we could not help him out with it, and he ultimately killed himself. A second was an anorexic girl. She stood five feet and seven inches tall and weighed at the last I saw her fifty-nine pounds. She literally starved herself to death believing that she was too fat and too ugly. Again, there was nothing I could do to stop her. Even though I committed her and tried every trick in the book to try to help her. The third was an individual whose two sons, ages ten and twelve, were killed by a drunk driver. The drunk driver was never prosecuted and was actually whisked out of the area after the accident. My client was so obsessed with this, he tried every way, shape, or form to get himself into court to have his story told. He wanted justice for the drunk driver. He would come into the office and say, "I just want to be with my boys, I just want to be with my boys."

We all knew what that meant. We all knew we could not stop him. On several occasions, he had made serious efforts to kill himself. We've been able to intervene and have him admitted to a hospital for evaluation. Finally, he took a double barrel shot gun, put it in his mouth, and blew his brains out. There was nothing anybody could do about that. I learned of this when he failed to keep an appointment and I called his home. His wife informed me what had happened. They had been married for twenty-one years.

I was often called after hours to respond to emergencies. I can remember one incident of an individual who had dropped off a bus, ended up in the local hospital emergency room having swallowed two bottles of aspirin. Needless to say, he didn't make it. He bled to death internally and there was nothing the doctors or anybody else could do to stop it. There was another one who dropped off a bus and had taken something called Angel Dust. As a result, he had decided to break up glass and ate several pieces of it. Of course, you know what happened. The glass cut his insides to ribbons and he also died from internal bleeding.

We had individuals who stuffed bananas up their rectums. One individual stuffed a coke bottle up his butt. One individual brought his wife in with a thirty-eight-revolver stuffed up her vagina. He brought her in to be committed even though he was the one who put the revolver there. The question was who really needed to be committed. The doctors were quite afraid to pull the revolver out because it was loaded and there could have been a serious accident. Fortunately, there was not. Anything that you can imagine, we saw.

The Flood and Federal Grants

I have lived a great portion of my life along the Susquehanna River. It is quite understandable that sooner or later, we would get flooded. The Susquehanna River flooded in 1936, in 1946, 1950, and in 1964. The major flood that I remember, the one that set the all-time record for floods concerning the Susquehanna River was in 1972, Hurricane Agnes.

Agnes had come up from the South and in from the East where it bumped into the Appalachian Mountains. It stalled there for several days. There was more than 15 inches of rain in three days. I was working in the local counseling service mental health agency in Lock Haven. Our office was located on West Main Street close to the banks of the Susquehanna River. We knew that we were in a flood zone. We knew that by listening to the radio and listening to the weather forecasters that we were going to be flooded. On June 21, 1972, my staff and I began to move things out of the office and up to the second floor of the house where we were located. We took typewriters, several drawers of case files, and other office equipment where they would not be threatened by the flood waters.

The next day, June 22, the river water went over its banks and record flood levels were set. For a couple of days, we couldn't go to the office because we were blocked by mud, debris, and water. While we couldn't get into our office and open it, I was asked to go around to several churches and assess the pianos that were damaged from the flood. I remember walking into the United Church of Christ where there were nine pianos. I opened up each one and watched the insides of the pianos fall out because all of the glue holding them together had been washed out by the food waters. I wrote appraisals totaling all of the pianos. None of them were salvageable. I also remember watching furniture flying out of houses on to the streets soaked and covered with mud.

We were able to open our office about three days after the flood. During the first day as we were cleaning up muddy floors and file cabinets, two representatives showed up from the Federal Government telling us that we were eligible for a Grant to repair the building. I applied for the Grant. For the next three years, I went through the bureaucratic process of answering all kinds of letters with regard to this Grant in order to receive the $12,000.00 we would be given to repair the building. I remember several times being referred to offices by people who swore they existed, only to find out that they did not. Finally, in 1975, I received a letter asking me to send a copy of our medical assistance license. I had already done these three times before.

I received a phone call saying the individual had a check that he wanted to send me for $12,000.00. By this time, our agency had been disbanded and we were being absorbed by another, which was the major mental health carrier of the area. The check was going to do us no good. When the individual told me about having the check and all that I needed to do was write a letter saying that I was willing to accept it, I told him that I was not prepared to write such a letter. His question was, "What should I do with this check?" My answer was, "The next time you go to the bathroom, take that check with you and use it accordingly." We never did get the check and never heard anything further from the Federal Government about it. I did have a file which was literally two feet thick containing all of the documents that accumulated from applying for this apparent federal grant. My advice to people in the future is to never apply for a Federal Grant!

Alcohol and Training Dogs

During my mental health career in the 1980s, we were charged with taking care of people who were addicted to drugs and/or alcohol. I had been working the evening shifts at our small clinic. One particular evening, a car pulled into the parking lot, a man got out, came in the door and stated that he was extremely frightened because he did not know where he had been for the past three days. He remembered that he had been released from jail. After that, he drew a blank until driving into our parking lot. I asked him if he had been taking drugs and he said no. I asked him if he had been drinking and he said yes and that he blacked out. My first question to him was, "Do you have any more alcohol in the car?" He said that he did. We walked out to the car, I reached into the back seat on the floor and pulled out two full bottles of pure grain alcohol. We took it inside to the clinic's kitchen. I said to him, "Pour this down the drain, or pour your life down the drain." He poured the pure grain alcohol down the drain. After admonishing him not to light up a cigarette for a while, until the alcohol had a chance to evaporate, I talked to him about what he wanted to do. That same evening, we sent him to a rehabilitation center where he stayed for the 28-day program. At the end of 28 days, he was released. I never saw him again, but I did hear later that he went south and ended up learning how to train guard dogs. He had a job working for a very wealthy family training their guard dogs and selling them. I don't know whether or not he fell of the wagon, but at least for a while, he had a good career and remained sober.

The Crying Man

My career in mental health was quite amazing. It's worth an entire book by itself if I could ever sit down and have the time to write it. Nobody would ever believe some of the experiences I've had. One that I vividly remember and is probably reflective of my style on how I did things, occurred when I was working at the Catholic Hospital in Williamsport in the early 1970s. It was a Friday afternoon at 4:30 PM. Our office usually closed at 5:00 PM. We were also responsible for after-hours emergency calls. Everybody was beginning to relax when an individual walked in who was crying. Obviously, he was upset so I, being the supervisor and director of the agency, asked one of my young staff members to sit down with the guy and find out what was going on.

After about 30 minutes, when we were ready to close the doors and go home, the young staff member came out and said, "This guy is continuing to cry, and I can't seem to get him to stop. I hate to send him home this way. We have no beds so we can't admit him to the hospital. You're the supervisor, it's your call. Would you take a look at him?" Reluctantly, I agreed to do so. I went into the office where he was, sat down in a chair opposite of him and introduced myself. I asked him, "What seems to be your problem?" His answer was, "I can't stop crying." I presented him with a question asking how long he had been crying. He returned with a reply saying he had been crying for three days. I asked him why he had been crying and he said, "I'm crying because I'm ugly." I looked at him and said, "My God...you've been ugly all your life. Why'd you wait till three days ago to start crying about it?"

Of course, you can guess what happened. The man became angry and hit the proverbial ceiling. He bounced around the room for about 20 minutes complaining about all kinds of things, including his treatment at work, his treatment at home, and just went on and on. He would not stop. When he finally paused to take a breath, I looked at him and said, "I noticed that you stopped crying." He looked at me and said, "How in the Hell did you do that?"

Goodbye Mental Health

I finally ended up getting out of mental health in 1985 when the agency I just joined went bankrupt. It was at that point

Barbara and I had both realized that our first love was music. It had always been music. Both of us had been told when we were younger there was no way we could make a living in music unless we wanted to teach in public schools as band or choral directors. We could not deny the fact that we loved music and she eventually began to successfully teach piano and I ran a music store.

We have spent the last thirty years operating a music store working with people and material that we both love. We have taught, we have kept books; we have sold instruments and accessories. We have performed. We have experimented in just about every segment of music including composing. Despite the successes we had in mental health and mental retardation social work, we finally arrived at our first love, and both of us knew it.

Chapter 9: Linda

Like everyone else my age those days, I wanted to live a normal life. I wanted to have the American Dream. I wanted a house, family, job, and more with a future to look forward too. As I mentioned previously, I did not date while in college. I didn't date much while I was working in the probation department until the end of my term. Linda's mother and my father worked at the same place. It was through that work situation that I met Linda, my first wife, the mother of my children.

She was in college at Lock Haven University as a Spanish major and was having difficulty with Math. Linda's mother asked me if I could help her. I said I could try, although I was not particularly strong in Mathematics. That's how we first met. Eventually, we decided to go to a movie for our first date. In retrospect, it was probably my first real date. I finished my tour at the probation department and applied for Graduate School. Linda graduated from Lock Haven University that same year. We drove to Pittsburgh for my interview with the School of Social Work. She also interviewed. My application was accepted, but hers was not.

Linda's Senior Year at Lock Haven State

After her graduation, she took a position with Warren County Pennsylvania Child Welfare Services because there were no positions available teaching Spanish. Our dating arrangement was a weekend affair. By the time we got to know each other fairly well, we would come home together to Lock Haven on the weekends. After a long time of doing this, I finally said to her that we needed to be together more of the time. She agreed and she accepted a position in Pittsburgh as a parole agent. In all fairness, she was not prepared for that job. She had been an only child, highly sheltered, and had no experience with the low-life element, unlike my experiences dealing with prisoners and other people of that ilk. It didn't go well for her as a parole agent.

I finished Graduate School and Linda stayed with parole. We took an apartment in Squirrel Hill, a nice neighborhood in the Pittsburgh area. By this time, we decided we would be married back home on June 11, 1966. She had some conditions. She wanted to make sure I had a job. I told her that was not a problem. I graduated Social Work School on a Friday and became a staff member at the same clinic that following Monday. She still had her parole agent job but was tempted to leave it. She met with many clients that frightened her and I don't blame her. Linda had to deal with many situations she was not prepared for as a parole agent.

Squirrel Hill was a predominately a Jewish community. Linda came home from the grocery store one evening complaining that she had been harassed by a number of people in the store. These people would, for instance block her path with a cart, push carts into her from behind, reach in front of her and grab items she intended to get and other such incidents. I should point out that we were the only

Christian family in our apartment building and with the name Bressler, which is German we were met with a great deal of suspicion.

In order to deal with this problem, I borrowed a white cane and a pair of sunglasses from a friend and went with Linda to the grocery store the next week. I had a great time playing blind man in a grocery store. As Linda pointed out to me each offender I would find a way to punish them. I ran into people with the cart, pushed carts from one end of the grocery store to the other end of the grocery store, deliberately ran into people, and so on.. In fact, I had a good time raising general hell in that store. The result was that no one bothered Linda from that day on. We decided we didn't want to rear children in the Pittsburgh area and wanted to come back to Lock Haven.

As we were getting ready to head back to Pittsburgh from a weekend visit in Lock Haven, Linda's father mentioned that the university wanted to initiate a Social Welfare Program and they were advertising for Social Workers. This was a Sunday evening and we needed to return for work the next day. Per her father's suggestion, I contacted the President of Lock Haven University. He told me he knew who I was because I had given a talk at his service club years earlier and remembered me. I told him my background and he said he was highly interested. He asked me to give him 15 minutes and then would call me back. When he did, he explained that I was to visit the chairman of the Social Sciences Department at his home for an interview; remember, this is still that Sunday evening that Linda and I had to get back to Pittsburgh for work the next morning. My first call to the president was at 6:30 PM. By 9:00 PM that same night, I had a contract to be an instructor of Social Work at Lock Haven University to begin the next fall semester in September 1967.

Linda and I had been married for a number of years. After I left the mental health field of work because of my own health, being overworked and a lack of sleep, we decided to open a bookstore in our hometown of Lock Haven. There was no such store there and felt this would serve a real community need. We got together with a book dealer in Williamsport, PA who set us up with books and magazines. We opened the store on a Saturday morning with the sun shining and a crowd of people ready to shop. We kept the bookstore from 1975 till 1977. In the course of that time, we also opened a music store. The bookstore was called The Knowledge Box and the music store next door The Music Box. We sold books, magazines, cards, etc. in the bookstore and pianos, organs, and other instruments in the music store.

Newspaper ad for the Knowledge Box

More than a year after we started, we moved our store into larger quarters further downtown. The justification was there would be more traffic leading to more business. Despite the move, the business was not doing well, and we needed to borrow money. My parents co-signed a loan for $50,000 against the advice from the bank to advance the business. Business continued to decline and in 1977, we decided one of us needed to go to work. Since I had a graduate degree and Linda did not, we decided that I was the one who would seek another job. Later that same year, I interviewed for a position in a town about 50 miles away from where we lived. The understanding was that if I secured that job, I would try it for about three to four months and would then decide what to do from there. My suggestion was that if the job went well, we would close the bookstore and move it and our family to the new town as I continued to work in the mental health agency in Lewisburg.

The three or four months passed, and it was time to make a decision. I had been living through the week in Lewisburg. I was living on a few dollars each week and rented a room. I ate out for most of my meals and started to lose a great deal of weight, but the job seemed to be going fairly well. I finally approached the subject with Linda, that it was time to decide if we were going to move. Some people in Lewisburg questioned if we were going to move the bookstore there. I thought it was a good idea because there was a university there and people were far more into intellectual pursuits than what we were experiencing in Lock Haven. Linda said that she didn't want to move.

I came home by bus one Friday evening as usual. I arrived at the bus station and Linda wasn't there. I called the house and told her I arrived. She said that the children were in bed. It was late in the evening and she didn't want to arouse them to pick me up, which meant I had to walk home. I walked approximately two miles to our home in Sunset Pines. When I arrived, I put my suitcase in the bedroom and sat down in the living room. I was very tired from the long walk while carrying my suitcase. Linda said to me, "If you give me the car, the house, $5,000.00 and the business, I will give you a divorce." I was shocked. I had no idea this was coming. She told me she spoke with three different attorneys before one finally agreed to take her case. The attorney who agreed to take her case was one that I knew from my days working in probation, and I said to her, "That attorney is going to help me more than he will help you." I was so shocked by everything that I couldn't sleep.

I got up after trying to get some rest and walked two miles back to downtown Lock Haven to an all-night greasy spoon type restaurant called the Texas Restaurant. I went in, sat down at the counter and proceeded to drink coffee while I tried to sort out what exactly was happening. I was there till about 5:00 AM, when the Hammermill Paper Company shift changed. A young man came up to me as I was in the throes of a very deep depression. He tapped me on the shoulder and said, "You may not remember me, but my name is Bill, and I was one of your probationers years ago when you worked at the juvenile court. I wanted you to know that everything turned out alright for me. I'm married, I'm working and have two children. I'm glad to see you again." This must have been God touching me in some way, telling me that I was a worthwhile person, and that I did make a difference in people's lives.

I walked back up to the house after daylight. Linda was not there. She had gone to visit her mother and took the children with her. There was nothing left for me to do but go back into town and catch the bus back to my job in Lewisburg. This was the beginning of a very difficult time for both me and Linda. I came home the next week and I said to her, "I don't think this is going to work out too well. You said you want a divorce; I think we should separate." We separated, I moved my things out with my brothers help and took them to my parent's house, which was halfway between Lock Haven and Lewisburg.

We remained separated for some time, which started in 1978. I would go to my parent's house on the weekends. They would pick up my children so that I could have visitations with them. I arranged payment of child support through our local domestic relations office. The separation was difficult. I had to rely on other people to see that I got to visit my kids. I never liked relying on other people and putting them out of their way. My parents were there to support me through the entire separation.

It was sometime between the start of our separation and the final declaration of divorce that I learned through a domestic relations complaint filed by Linda that she was in the hospital and had been diagnosed with Multiple Sclerosis.

I immediately offered to return home. We could call this whole thing off and find a way to straighten things out. Linda said no and that she didn't want me to return home. She had rented another house after selling the house in Sunset Pines. I was left with the financial burden because the bookstore was not making money and I had a salary. I made payments against the loan my parents co-signed for us of $365.00 a month, plus the costs of my room, eating out and paid for my visits with my children. I was taking a financial bath and I knew it, but there was no other way. I was 40 years old, in debt up to my eyeballs on a limited income and living in an unfamiliar town. I had no real friends except for people I knew from work. It was the end of the world as far as I was concerned. I didn't think there was ever going to be a way out of it. Our divorce was finalized on Valentine's Day, February 14, 1979. To this day, I consider the fact that I did recover, and things got better, as a kind of miracle.

As time passed and things settled down after the divorce, I had some time to think over my situation. I was the first member of my family to get a divorce. That singled me out however, it turned out that my youngest brother was also going through the divorce process at the same time. I had some company in my misery. I began to grieve the loss of my marriage. I didn't know how things were going go or work out. I was financially strapped; I was alone and thought it was the end of the world. I didn't know who my friends were and who were my enemies. It turned out some people I thought to be my friends were not. They were highly critical of me. I guess that was their right. There were others I did not expect who turned out to be really good friends; well beyond what I could have imagined. In thinking over the situation, I don't wish to lay blame on anybody. One of the things that's very easy to do this day and age, whether it's politics, religion, divorce, whatever, is to play the blame game. I find this to be absolutely useless. To this day, I don't know exactly what went wrong in my first marriage. It wasn't all bad. We had many good times. I remember two summers when we went to the beach for vacation. The first summer Cindy was barely a year old. It was great fun having her on the beach watching her eat sand and do other random things. We had other good times. We had many fine experiences. Our days in the college faculty were very rewarding. We were entertained at a number of galas as well as having to perform some entertaining of our own. We were living the highlife in many ways.

What we realized...

Years later, Linda and I had an understanding and a kind of reckoning of the ways. We concluded that one of the problems was the disease that she ultimately succumbed to. Both of us wondered if her affliction lingered before she was diagnosed with Multiple Sclerosis. I can think of several episodes that she would go to the doctor for one illness or another with no diagnosis forthcoming. She had symptomatic complaints before we separated, mainly "lightening" in her eyes. No one associated this with anything serious. Perhaps her disease was a factor. Another thought was Linda's close relationship with her mother. One might say too close. This presented with a great deal of conflict between us. I learned later when we discussed the idea of Linda and the kids moving to Lewisburg, her mother threw quite a guilt trip on her. This, as remembered by my daughter. I know that she was conflicted about the divorce because while she had attempted to see attorneys and told me she wanted a divorce, she actually also told me she didn't want one.

Perhaps a factor was when Linda insisted that we go to a doctor and have them explain my visual condition was not hereditary. I told her several doctors had already explained this and that I was absolutely certain my limited sight was not hereditary. Nonetheless, before she would consent to marriage, we needed to go to the doctor to satisfy her curiosity.

Another thought was Linda's mother's absolute insistence that I go check out the possibility of 20/20 vision and her willingness to pay. She paid nearly $2,000.00 for our expenses, which was a pretty large sum of money in 1969, especially for a widow. I have to conclude on the basis of this and several other remarks that were made, both by Linda and her mother during our marriage, that my vision problem was in fact a difficulty in our marriage. To be fair about it, Linda was left with a great deal of responsibility. She had to do all of the driving. She had to read all of the correspondence. She had to do most of the housework. For example, I could not safely mow a yard without having all kinds of accidents. She was left to do many household tasks. She took it upon herself to pay all bills and write checks. At that time, there were no technologies to assist with such endeavors. This left her with a great deal of responsibility, maybe more than what she wanted to have.

In speaking with a number of blind and partially sighted friends, several of whom went through divorces, all were married to fully sighted people, and the marriages did not last. I have to conclude that this was something of a problem and that it had some legitimacy for my ex-wife Linda. We had many good conversations trying to figure out what went wrong, what we could have changed, but it was over. I was remarried and established a new life in Lewisburg. There was no going back.

As time passed and I started to work in my music store, Linda and I talked on the phone many times. I discovered that she liked a candy called Swedish Fish, which was pretty much all sugar. Whenever my children would come to visit, I often sent a box of Swedish Fish along home for their mother.

November 23, 1992

I remember the night in 1992 when I received a phone call from my son. He told me his mother suddenly passed away. The feeling that went through me was indescribable. I found myself grieving immensely for her and feeling bad for my children. My son was 19 and my daughter was 22. I learned that my daughter was pregnant out of wedlock. My son was attempting to study at college but was also having issues with alcohol. I felt helpless being unable to do anything for them. I was 50 miles away and couldn't drive. I didn't have a way to get to them on a regular basis. I couldn't move them into my house, and they didn't really want to do that.

My son called me a few days after his mother's funeral and said, "Don't worry dad. I have a solution." I asked him what it was. He said he went to see the recruiter. I asked my son what he told them, and he said, "I told them that I was messed up. My mother had died, and I didn't know what to do from here. I need help." I was curious to what the recruiter's response was to that; according to my son, he simply said, "Sign here." By January 1993, just two months after Linda had passed away, he was on his way to basic training in Fort Knox, KY. My daughter remained in the house that Linda and my kids lived in however, discovered the mortgage had not been paid and the house was going to get repossessed by the bank. She had to fend for herself in some other way. She relocated with her boyfriend to his hometown. Their relationship did not last; they split up, leaving my daughter to be in the status of single parent. My children ultimately started their adult lives in dire difficulty, and I felt I had not been much of a parent to them for allowing this to happen.

Letters to my children

Chapter 10: Becoming a Father

Linda and I were married on June 11, 1966. I started to work at the University of Pittsburgh in the psychiatric clinic as a therapist. We rented an apartment in Squirrel Hill, a Jewish neighborhood of Pittsburgh. This proved to be quite an interesting place. We always came home to Linda's parents on the weekends in our brand new 1966 Plymouth Fury. Linda didn't want to spend the weekends in Pittsburgh. I started my position as an instructor in 1967 at Lock Haven University with the idea that I would help establish an undergraduate program in Social Work; the very program from which my son graduated from over fifty years later. We bought a house and moved back to Lock Haven.

We were married four years and our first child came along. We were always asked, "When are you going to start a family?" In fact, society pressures young couples to do this. I finally got sick of all the questions to the point when people asked us about starting a family, I began to respond by telling people, "We don't know what to do." That usually stopped the questions about starting a family. Early in 1970, we discovered that Linda was pregnant with our first child. After a long nine months, she was born on September 1, 1970. We named her Cynthia Lee. No-one can describe how it was to have your first child. Here I was, a partially blind person that struggled to gain access to a successful career throughout my life. I fought my way into jobs and was turned down from others. I wanted to live the American Dream. I was married, we had purchased a house, and our first child was now here. All of this was the beginning of that dream life. I always wanted to live in the sighted world despite my lack of eyesight. I felt that was the way the world was, and I needed to adjust to it. No one can describe the thrill of your first child. I sat in the hospital waiting room waiting for them to come out and tell me she was delivered. She weighed over 8 pounds and 5 ounces. In 1970, fathers were not allowed in the delivery room. We were not allowed to hold our child. We weren't even allowed to see the child until sometime later. I was ecstatic. The thought that my flesh and blood had somehow come into this world. This baby was a part of me and a part of her mother. That's the ultimate creation. No one, I think, can ever experience that in the same way again as it happens with the first born. Oh yes, you do experience it if you have other children, but it's not quite the same. The first born is probably the greatest thrill of all because it means that you have been able to produce a child.

The second child is exactly that; the second child. Cynthia was nearly three years old when our second offspring came along. The doctor told Linda all through her pregnancy that she was going to have another little girl. We had a beautiful name chosen, Karen Lynn. Our second child came along on July 12, 1973 weighing nine pounds. The doctor came out and said to me, "Congratulations. You have a son, and he is almost as big as you are!" We named him Richard Samuel. This was a name that we had picked previously in case the doctor was wrong.

That was another kind of thrill. Not the same as the first born, but now, I not only have a daughter, but I had what every man wants to have, a son. Linda originally wanted to name him after me. I said I didn't want a junior. His name is a combination of names in our family; Richard, my middle name and Samuel, one of his grandfather's middle names. This satisfied everyone. Years later, Rick told me that he wished I had named him Richard Christopher. I told him jokingly, "You didn't tell me that at the time we named you, so I named you Richard Samuel."

Watching my children grow is an immense experience. It was part of what I thought was the American Dream. There were no problems during either pregnancy. Both children were born healthy and ideally as you would want. We could not have had it any better than when the children had arrived and begun to grow.

A very young Cindy and Rick

Chapter 11: My Children

Cindy

My daughter Cynthia was born on September 1, 1970, at 6:18 pm. Her mother spent the entire day in labor with me waiting around for her to be born. Linda's mother and I hung out in the waiting room. Cindy finally arrived. We took her home five days later. From day one she was a good baby by definition. Within two weeks she slept the whole night through on a regular basis. She gave no particular problems, never got sick, was pleasant, and didn't cry a great deal except when she needed changed or fed. By the time Cindy was two or three years old, it was obvious that she was going to be a pretty good child. She listened, behaved well, did everything her parents asked her to do, and she didn't complain. By the time she went to school, it was obvious how she was going to turn out. She was everybody's caretaker and problem solver. In fact, I remember a story from her Kindergarten class. She decided in the middle of class to help one of her little friends with an assignment that her friend couldn't do. The teacher saw she was talking to the other student and trying to help. Her teacher asked Cindy what she was doing. Cindy replied that she was solving a problem. She told the teacher, "After all, you told us when there was a problem, we should solve it. We're just solving a problem."

As she grew, she was the primary caretaker of her mother when she fell ill. She progressed into becoming a case worker for the STEP program and finally, she became a nurse. This was no surprise to me. Nursing is the ultimate caretaker profession. As a nurse, her current job is taking care of an autistic child. Sometimes her client may have behavior problems, but as she points out, I raised two boys that had problems, so it doesn't bother me much. This on top of careers working in a prison or in nursing homes. She has always been a champion for the underdog and indeed, when her brother was going through his problems, she was there to help take care of him. In addition to all I've said so far, she has already told me, "Dad…if anything happens, you are not going to a nursing home. I will arrange to take care of you myself." I might add that she also took care of her grandmother, which was no easy task, given the fact that the grandmother had become rather obstreperous.

My daughter was expecting her first baby at age 22. The pregnancy was out of wedlock and I felt that the man she was involved with didn't have much of a future. He had no high school diploma, no driver's license, no steady job, and yet Cindy insisted that he was a kind and generous person. As it turned out, I later on learned that indeed he was. He did help immensely in taking care of my ex-wife during the latter part of her sickness and until her death. Cindy did eventually decide that this was the man she didn't want to marry, even having lived with him for some time. Later on, she became involved with another guy whom I didn't think much of either. This one she did marry and had two boys with him: James and Damian. That marriage did not last long as her husband was not true to her and was involved with other people. He had several marriages beyond the one with my daughter. Cindy later admitted the marriage was abusive. In fact, during this dark time, she felt like the underdog and her brother was her champion. Rick was her strength when she was uncertain on how her life would move forward.

Cindy married later again to a man she met at work. She did not bare any children to him but helped him rear his children along with her own. This marriage lasted for some 15 years. At the end of that time, Cindy decided it was time for her to grow. She was interested in Nursing and managed to get herself into Nursing school, which she completed in 2012. The marriage did not last and ended in divorce, primarily initiated by Cindy, who felt that things were going nowhere and that her husband again was not being true to her. Since that time, she has married again, this time to her high school sweetheart; the one whom she said broke her heart when he left her after high school. He too had been married before and had a divorce and two children. Cindy has always had the idea of blending a family together. No matter who she was involved with, they were always included as part of her family, whether they were her stepchildren or not. Today, Cindy is a successful Licensed Practical Nurse and takes care of an autistic child on a regular basis. This, after a rather difficult life, raising her children, and going through husbands who were not faithful to her. As I have said before, Cindy is the consummate caretaker. This is probably what she will do all of her life.

Dick and baby Cindy

A Story About Cindy

When I took the mental health job in 1972 at the hospital in Williamsport, PA, my wife located a house near the hospital that was for sale. It was a stucco house with corner windows. We were able to buy it. It had a very nice yard and the house had very spacious rooms. It was walking distance to work which of course was very nice for me.

Our next-door neighbor was an advocate for flowers. He loved flowers and raised them in beautiful flower beds. One day as we were out in the yard, the neighbors were out too. We were socializing. My two-year-old daughter was out with us and playing in the yard. She wandered over to the neighbor's yard and picked two or three of his flowers. She brought them over and handed them to me. I thanked her and told her that was very nice, but if she wanted to pick Mr. Glosser's flowers, she should ask him first. She wandered away again and pretty soon returned with more flowers. I said to her, "Did you ask Mr. Glosser?" She shook her head no. I told her that Daddy was getting angry with her. She looked at me quite innocently and said, "You'll get over it."

Rick

On July 12, 1973, Linda was outside weeding. She had an unbelievable burst of energy. She was pulling weeds from the flower beds as if there was no tomorrow. At about 6:30 pm, she insisted that it was time to go to the hospital. She was having labor pains. We made it to the hospital and at 7:43 pm, my son Richard Samuel arrived in this world. I was not allowed in the delivery room nor anybody else. Rick was the opposite of his sister. He was lively and constantly testing limits as he grew. He was a child who was very busy.

He would just go and go and go. He would run and play and carry on and suddenly, he would become quiet. We wouldn't know where he was. I would go through the house searching for him and often find him passed out on the floor sound asleep. Frequently I would pick him up and put him to bed in his clothes. He would sleep the whole night through and the next day, we would go through the entire process again.

Rick was a student from the time he was a little boy. He actually seemed to enjoy school and he did well in school. He got good grades. As he got older, he became interested in art. We would see him drawing cartoons, which he often watched early in the morning. At my house, he would often get up so early that the streetlights were still on. He was an expert at video games. One night, he asked if he could play Pac Man before he went to bed. Not realizing what an expert he was at playing it, I told him yes. He played the game and just kept winning over and over again until it was past his bedtime. I did catch on and eventually had to stop letting him play video games by a certain time in the evening. Rick liked testing people's limits. He had a temper, was cute, and he knew it. He would frequently go into the kitchen and compliment his stepmother on the meals she was preparing. Everybody liked Rick. He was an outgoing personality from day one.

After the death of his mother, he joined the Army in 1993. This was two months after his mother had passed away. For over two years, he served his country and was ultimately sent to Vicenza, Italy for his overseas duty assignment. In 1995, he was discharged from the Army under some cloud of problematic behavior regarding substance abuse. He came home and took a job in the Lock Haven area and got an apartment. Shortly after he had come home, his sister Cindy came to my store on a visit and told me that her brother had lost his apartment. He came to her home 28 miles away along the Susquehanna River. At her house, he detoxed himself from various substances. This was quite dangerous.

She said that she and her grandparents did not know what to do and needed help. I was a social worker and was familiar with substance abuse issues and mental health treatment. They felt I was the one to come to for help. I have to say that I was being somewhat facetious. These were the same grandparents whom I was told regarded me as the blackest hearted S O B in the area and now coming to me for help. I told Cindy that the first thing they needed to do was not give her brother any more money. She said they would not do this. I then told her that if they wanted me to solve this problem, they need to do what I say. They could give him clothing, they could pay rent or pay a bill, but don't give him money. He would only drink it up or buy drugs with it. Rick had told his sister he knew he needed help and he was ready to accept it.

He was brought down to me at my home where I arranged for him to meet with a drug and alcohol facility in our area to discuss treatment options. Rick, by his own admission said that he needed 24/7 help. He didn't think outpatient supervision would be enough. He chose to enter a 28-day rehabilitation program and did very well. After the 28 days, he came out of the program and came to live in the same town as I did. I secured an apartment for him in the same building where my store was located. Our church graciously provided his first month's rent. I spoke to a local gas station owner who gave him a third shift job at his business.

Rick was on his own. He was expected to attend AA or NA meetings and to participate in other activities in association with drug and alcohol rehabilitation. During the course of his time before his stay at rehab and getting clean, he had accumulated several fines and other problems, which he actually didn't remember. We began to receive phone calls. One from New Jersey, another from the area of Lock Haven where he was living before getting clean. I agreed to pay the fines for him with the understanding that it was a loan and that he would work off the fines. I gave my son what was probably for me the most difficult lecture I have ever given anybody in my life. I told him that he came out of rehab, that he had been told that he had the disease of addiction. He had learned how to manage it. I explained to him that within a few blocks of where he was living, there was a State Store and several bars and taverns. I told him that I could not supervise him 24 hours a day seven days a week and guarantee the prevention that he would not go to the bars or the taverns. He learned a great deal on how to work through his struggles and manage his behavior. I told him that if he did not do so and went back to using various substances like before, I would have nothing more to do with him. I was not going to get gray hair constantly bailing him out of trouble. He assured me that he had enough and that he fully intended to remain clean. He came down and worked at my store earning commission on products that he sold and thereby paid me back the fines and in fact, to his credit, he insisted on doing that. My demanding it was not necessary.

During the course of his stay in our area and working in my store, I purchased what was called a Suzuki SP-8 Digital Workstation; a keyboard that had hundreds of digitally sampled sounds. Since Rick's apartment was a few floors above the store, he would come down to the store late at night and play around with the keyboard. He began composing and scoring numerous musical pieces using the digital workstation. The music, the compositions, and the keyboard were great therapy and were instrumental in his recovery. It turns out that my son is quite musically talented. He wrote several excellent pieces and orchestrated them using the keyboard in very unique and creative ways.

My son's recovery began and I'm happy to say is a success. Almost 25 years have passed, and he has remained abstinent. He is now married, has two children, has a good job and successful career. No one knows how happy it makes me to have seen my son make such a great recovery. I'd like to think that my expression of tough love might have had some positive influence on his successful recovery.

To this day, Rick is personable and also likes helping others. He, like his older sister, obtained his nursing license and in December 2019, after many years of hard work, he earned his Bachelor of Science in Social Work from Lock Haven University. He was then accepted into a graduate program at Edinboro University where within one year, he will receive his master's degree having been awarded advanced standing in the program. Rick graduated Magna Cum Laude; a pure unadulterated feat when you consider that he was working full time, raising a family, was going to school, and was also producing a film since he become quite a talent doing video type work. His 32-minute documentary film was shown at our local theatre and as a fund-raiser in his hometown. In addition to this, he also wrote a book that was subsequently published after having done a magnanimous research job about a WWII Ace Pilot that crashed a plane after the war in our local area.

Rick at age 19 during Basic Training

A Story About Rick

We were living in Lewisburg and I had just been remarried to Barbara. My son and daughter had come down for a weekend visit. There was a vacant lot next to our house and we had purchased my son a bicycle. He was about six years old. He wanted to learn how to ride his bike. I spent the day with him out in the vacant lot trying to show him how to ride bike. He would go a little bit and upset, then he would cry. He'd get up, get back on the bicycle, go again, upset and then cry. This went on for about half of that afternoon. Finally, he began to get the hang of it and balance the bike quite nicely. He stopped and decided to take a break until after supper.

We went in the house and my daughter Cindy then asked if I would go on a bike ride with her now that I was finished showing Rick how to ride. I told her I would. Immediately, Rick said, "I want to go along." I told him no. I didn't feel like he could ride well enough yet to do that. Cindy and I took off on our bikes and went for a ride. Rick lost his temper. He went into the house and told his stepmother that he was going to smash his bicycle and never ride it again. His step-mother told him that if he did that, he probably wouldn't get another bicycle, "You might want to think about it," she said. He became very angry, went up to the top of the stairs, sat down, and waited for me to come home.

When I came home, he was at the top of the steps, becoming very angry, and giving me the business about not taking him along for a bike ride. I finally told him he could simply stay at the top of the stairs till he decided to quit crying and get over being mad; then he could come down. In about 30 seconds, he asked if he could come down telling me that he wasn't angry anymore. I said he could. He came down the steps and sat down beside his stepmother. Suddenly, he caved in and fell asleep with his head in her lap.

Chapter 12: I Didn't See You There

The Purple Coat

In 1977, I came to work in a small town along the banks of the Susquehanna River called Lewisburg. I worked there in a mental health counseling service dealing with outpatient people and was the clinical supervisor of the staff. One of the staff members that I came to know and became very good friends with had a wife who also worked in the same town but, in a bank just up the street from our office. Every day, when lunch time came, I would walk up the street to my favorite deli and get something to eat.

As this friend of mine and I became close, his wife began to decide she would tease me having to do with my low vision. She always wore a purple coat and each day I would go out to lunch and she was working, she would come out of the bank at the same time. We would be walking towards each other in the street and she would get right up on top of me and say, "Oh excuse me sir. I didn't see you there."

This one day came, we were getting ready to go to lunch. I went out, started up the street and I saw at some distance the purple coat and I decided, "This time I would turn the tables on her." I came up to the person with the purple coat. She walked straight up in front me as my friend Pam always did. When she got within three feet of me, I reached out and grabbed her and said, "Okay, I got you this time Pam." A strange voice came out and said to me, "You certainly did." Obviously, this was not Pam. I said to the woman, "I'm not even going to try and explain this."

The Gentleman

There was a time when Linda and I went shopping. My children were little, and someone was babysitting them while we went out. We came into a clothing store; one of the larger ones in town. My wife drifted over to where the women's clothing was, and I decided to look around another section of the store.

I found my way into what was probably the men's section and was walking along down one of the aisles. Suddenly, this gentleman appeared in front of me. I almost ran into him. I stepped to the left. He stepped in the same direction I did. I shifted and stepped to the right. He stepped the same way. I did this three or four times and kept saying, "Excuse me, excuse me." Finally, I reached out to push him the opposite direction that I wanted to go. When I did, I got a fist load of full-length mirror.

Letters to my children

Chapter 13: See Dick Drive...

The Cornfield and "Frankentruck"

People have often asked me, "Have you ever attempted to drive?" I don't have enough vision to procure a driver's license. The answer is, "Yes!" I have attempted to drive on four different occasions as I recall. The first time was on our family farm during the summer before my first year of college.

My father was a tremendous mechanic in those days. He could put a vehicle together with scotch tape and baling wire. He had the habit of taking old cars, cutting them down and turning them into pick-up trucks. The pick-up truck we had was one which he had created. It had no cab. The gas tank was the front seat with the spout coming up between the driver and the passenger. The vehicle was open all the way back to the truck bed, which dad had placed on it. We used that vehicle around the farm.

One day, my brother and I were to go and pick sweet corn from the field which we had planted the year before.

We would drive between two rows. My brother would reach out the driver's side and pick off ears of corn from the stock as we drove by, as I would reach out the passenger's side doing the same, with both of us chucking them back into the truck bed. It was a neat process. We picked the entire field that way. When we were at the far end of the field for the last time, my brother asked me if I'd like to try and drive the old truck. I simply said, "Sure."

He showed me how to shift gears and use the clutch. We started from the far end of the field. We put the old truck in low gear, and I began to drive heading back towards the barn. As we got near the barn, my brother started to repeatedly tell me to slow down. I didn't know how to slow down. He didn't think to show me how to do that. I didn't know to push in the clutch and shift the gear into neutral while applying the brake. We didn't stop. We continued up the barn hill and were heading for the barn floor, as we came upon the chicken house, I side swiped it knocking it over off its foundation of four blocks, tearing up the one side badly. We headed from there to the barn hill. My brother dived across and turned off the truck's ignition, kicked my foot off of the accelerator and shifted the gears. By that point, we were inside the barn, almost ready to go beyond the barn floor.

Our parents were working at the time. We had 30 minutes to fix the chicken house so no one would notice anything happened. Carefully, we put the boards back together the best we could and nailed them fast. We couldn't do anything about the fact that the chicken coop was moved over to the extreme end of the cement blocks that once were its foundation.

A few days later, we were hauling logs for our dad and pulling them in to be sawed up. As we came around the corner and went into the barn for lunch, dad was riding along with us. He noticed that the chicken house was moved over on the foundation. He said to my brother, "You got a little close with that first log didn't you." My brother said yes, and dad never knew, until at least a year later, that his eldest son had attempted to drive the truck and nearly caused a serious accident.

The Golden Mustang

In 1964, I was dating Linda. We had barely met and gone on a date. She came over to pick me up from my family farm. It was in the summer. She had gone to work and had just purchased a brand-new Mustang Coupe. It was gold and one of the first Mustangs that were made that had a 6-cylinder engine with a stick shift. She began to tease me about driving since she knew I was not a licensed driver. She did mention that it would be neat if I could drive and asked if I wanted to try and drive the Mustang. I told her it was a bad idea. She laughed it off and said, "Oh let's try it anyway."

We climbed in the Mustang, put it in low gear, let the clutch out gradually, hit the accelerator slightly and started to head out my parent's driveway. Our driveway led to a State Road it intersected with. Across the state road was a ditch that led into the woods. I made the turn entirely too wide because I couldn't judge depth and distance very well. The right front wheel of the Mustang went into the ditch and there we sat. It took both of my younger brothers to get the car out. Fortunately, no damage was done to the car. We weren't going that fast when I put it in the ditch. I thought that might have been the end of my dating Linda, but it turned out otherwise. She said, "You warned me not to have you drive. It's my own fault." Gratefully, I agreed with her.

God's Grace and Temporary Vision

Christmas Eve of 1990, we were at my parents' home, where they had lived since 1954. My brother, his wife and children were there, along with me and my children. My nephew Tim said to me, "Let's go for a drive Uncle Dick. You can drive my truck." My brother, Tim's dad, and everybody else immediately said no, no, no. That's a bad idea. Even I agreed with them, but between my son and my nephew, they wanted me to try it. Finally, I said, "Okay. You have to be my co-pilots." They agreed that they would.

I sat in the driver's seat, with my nephew just to my right and my son on the far right of the passenger seat. We came out of the driveway and made a left turn to get on the road with Tim's help. We drove for six miles to the town of Loganton. It was pretty much a straight road making it easy for me since I didn't have to make any turns. Along the way, my nephew and son would both guide me by telling me to merge left or right depending on if I were getting too close to the middle of the road, or too close to take out a mailbox or two. We made it an entire six miles with no problems; all the way to Loganton.

We were soon going to approach an intersection in Loganton where I needed to make a left turn, cross the Valley, with the intention of going back to my parent's house on the other side of the valley. When we made it to the intersection, I began to think that making turns was not the easiest thing for me to do and thought about having my nephew make the turn for me, but he and my son said to just go ahead, and we'll see that you get through the turn.

I started the left-hand turn. Down the road just up ahead, I saw lights coming from the opposite direction and I panicked. What does one do when one panics? One braces himself. That's exactly what I did; I braced myself but did so with my foot on the gas pedal. With the truck in low gear, we tore out of the intersection and started to head for a garage on the right side of us. By God's grace, I swear I saw the garage, and sharply turned the steering wheel left to avoid hitting the cinder blocked building which then had the out-of-control truck with me as the pilot heading straight for a cemetery with many plots and large memorial stones. Again, God's grace gave me temporary sight, allowing me to the see the quickly approaching large marble memorials and I swerved quickly back to the right and avoided hitting them. A car was coming from the opposite direction and passed us as I nearly swiped the side of it, again, while avoiding the memorials.

Finally, we got stopped, but it was not because of my skilled driving and my applying the brake pedal. It was a large telephone pole. The entire right front portion of my nephew's truck looked like twisted metal. Even though we were stopped, my foot was still on the accelerator making the truck spin around the pole like trying to make donuts in a parking lot. My nephew managed to get my foot off of the gas pedal, got the truck to stop and he hopped out. He immediately went to the people in the other car we nearly hit since they stopped to make sure they were okay and not hurt. Needless to say, the woman was panicked. Tim managed to calm her down and get her on the way. Miraculously, Tim got the truck turned around and we all piled back in and went to his house, which was only about one mile from where the accident happened. In case you were curious, I did not make the drive to my nephew's house.

When we arrived, we called my parents' house and let them know what happened and that nobody was seriously hurt, although my son did bash his head with some force on the windshield. At that time, his mother and I were divorced. When he went back home to Lock Haven that night, he was having some dizzy spells. His mother took him to the local hospital's emergency room where they discovered that he did have a mild concussion. When I asked him what he told them at the hospital after they asked what happened, he told them he had fallen down a flight of stairs. I asked him, "Why did you tell them that?" His answer was priceless; he said to me, "Did you want me to tell them that I was riding around in a pick-up truck with my blind father driving?"

What strikes me funny about this is the story of what happened when my nephew called his insurance company about the accident. Of course, he was not going to tell them that his partially blind uncle was behind the wheel and caused the wreck. The story that he did tell them was so absurd that the insurance company had to believe it.

The story that he gave them was that he stopped at the stop sign. Started around the turn to the left. As he came around the turn, he saw two dogs in the middle of the road screwing. He swerved to miss them and lost control of the truck with the grand finale of striking the telephone pole. The insurance company bought the story and basically covered the damages. This is a story that I've never forgotten, and every time I see my nephew Tim, he reminds of that cold Christmas Eve from nearly 30 years ago.

Old Marge, a Local Girl, and a Joy Ride

Not all of my driving escapades involved an automobile or some other type of vehicle. One involved a horse and a buggy. There was a young woman down the road from us at a neighboring farm who was about my age. I met her as we attended the same church. We both could sing and would often sing duets in church. She knew that I had horses and kept begging me to take her on a horse and buggy ride.

I finally promised that I would. I suggested that she come out to my house, have dinner, and then we could go for the horse and buggy ride. She agreed.

She had a brand new 1960 yellow Chevrolet. She worked for a local newspaper in a town about 30 miles away. It was a good job, and it did in fact enable her to buy the car. I wanted a ride in this car in the world's worst way.

She came to my house the night we agreed on and we had a nice dinner. A half hour or so after we ate, I got Old Marge out and hitched her up to my rubber tired yellow and black buggy that had an open top. We climbed aboard and we rode for about a mile and a half to a gravel bank which was near our house. There was a road that curved around it.

As we came to the gravel bank and I took the curved road, we got to the far side and Old Marge realized that she was heading towards home. Suddenly, she took the bit in her teeth and took off at a gallop. There was no stopping her. I pulled on the reigns and tried to see saw them. The horse kept going full tilt. I never knew Old Marge could run that fast. We flew down the road heading towards home. My concern was that if we turned too sharply into our driveway, the buggy would upset. Buggies are not made to go around sharp turns at a fast pace. The horse must have realized this too because she took the turn by the driveway at a diagonal instead of a sharp turn.

The buggy rolled into the yard. I told the girl to duck her head because I realized we were approaching my mother's clothing lines. We ducked down and the horse headed right for the barn. The gate was opened to the barn yard. Old Marge went through the gate, but the buggy was too wide to make it through. We hit the fence on either side of the gate and knocked both front wheels off of the buggy. I never did get a ride in that 1960 yellow Chevrolet!

Chapter 14: The Interest in Music

My interest in music dates back to my early childhood; as early as two or three years old. My parents used to tell me when I was around three, every day at dinner time, I would go to our old Philco floor model radio, turn it on and turn the dial until I found a certain radio station that played country music. I can remember as a preschooler listening to several different radio programs in the evening, especially during the winter season and when it got dark early. This was when radio reception improved immensely. One of my favorite programs then was called, "The Supper Time Frolic," and it was broadcast from WJJD out of Chicago, IL. Another was WCKY out of Cincinnati, OH which was also a country music station that broadcast every night. An even more enjoyable radio program was WWVA from Wheeling, WV, The Jamboree, which was broadcast every Saturday night and featured top country stars of the day.

When I was about three, my father bought me a fluto-phone and I learned quite quickly how to play it. I could play simple tunes on it. By the time I went to blind school, we began piano lessons. I took piano lessons through about six grades. In addition, when I reached 4th grade, I took violin lessons and played in the school orchestra.

During the summer of my 6th or 7th grade years, my parents entered me in several amateur contests. I won them all as a singer. Word of this got back to my music teacher at school, probably from my parents. He talked to me about joining his church choir, where he was an assistant organist at a rather large Episcopal church in downtown Pittsburgh. I went and auditioned for the choir and made it as a boy soprano. I was able to hit a sixth octave C with no trouble. We sang very complicated and classical sacred music. I sang with the choir for two years before my voice changed and I had to quit. We were paid to sing in that choir. In addition to the joy of singing, I made pretty good earnings by getting paid $0.50 for every rehearsal, two each week, and $0.75 to sing on Sundays. I earned nearly $2.00 a week to sing in that choir, which was big money for a 12-year-old boy in those days.

When I reached high school, I was playing slide trombone and participated in the school's marching band as well as our school's dance band. At the end of my junior year in high school, in 1955, our band traveled to Cleveland, OH, and played at the International Kiwanis Convention. When

I came out of high school, I played with a country music band at home during the summer and we played on the local radio station WBPZ in Lock Haven.

Dick playing trombone with the band

I've mentioned learning how to tune pianos while in blind school previously. It did a lot more for me than what I could have ever guessed when I started college. I was the only person at Penn State who was ever able to invade a sorority suite legally because of them asking me to tune their piano. Piano tuning continued to serve me after I graduated college because it was my one source of income I could earn while

I was looking for employment. It was good money for someone my age with my circumstances.

By the time I got to graduate school, I had become a pretty proficient guitar player thanks to how much I learned previously while at Penn State. By the mid-1960s, Coffee Houses began to surface everywhere in Pittsburgh, which enabled me to perform at several different ones as a guitar player/folk singer. I also started getting requests from people to teach them how to play guitar. I ended up having several students.

When I completed graduate school, I continued tuning pianos on a regular basis and kept playing. While I was on the faculty at Lock Haven University, I played at coffee houses and picked up some guitar students. Up to this point in my life, music has served me well. It gave me the ability to make money and I developed a hobby in music. Over the course of several years, I taught myself how to play multiple instruments; including banjo, mandolin, guitar, some fiddle, bass guitar and even the vibraharp (similar to a xylophone). I was rather proficient in music, probably much more than the average person.

My music career continued on through my life. If you remember, I mentioned in another section that my first wife and I opened a music store in 1975 and called it the Music Box. I have to say that we did not know much about the music business, I just knew that I could play and teach. The store only lasted until 1977. We learned a little something about the rough edges of the music business. We had obtained a franchise in pianos and organs from the Thomas Organ Company; however, we received a registered letter less than a year later saying that the Thomas Organ Company franchise territory had been awarded to another music store in town. This meant that we had to sell out what inventory we had at substantial price reductions.

It was at this point in which we realized that our bookstore/music store combination was not going to work very well and didn't earn enough money. I was then in a situation where I needed to return to social work.

In 1985, I was working at a small counseling service when I was recruited by another for more money and better hours. After interviewing for the position, I accepted the job and went to work for an agency called Life Care Counseling. They did mental health counseling for people of all walks of life. I had worked for the agency for about four weeks. On Monday morning, the beginning of the fifth week, I went to work and discovered that the desks were gone, the chairs were gone, the files were gone, the phones were gone, and the entire office was empty. I would have felt pretty foolish, but the same thing happened to 30 other employees who worked for that agency. It meant that I was out of work and owed three weeks of pay, which I never did get. We learned that the company went bankrupt. They had never procured their licenses to operate and ran out of money.

Over the next five years, I applied for several positions that were available, but was refused every one of them. The ostensible reason was, "You can't drive, and this job requires a lot of driving." The second reason was, "You're over-qualified. You probably won't stay with us." It was pretty clear to me that the real reason was, "You have visual problems and we really don't trust that." Even some friends of mine whom I contacted to see if there was some possibility for work, people that I had gone to graduate school with and kept in contact with, suddenly could not help me in any way shape or form.

Through the struggles of trying to find a job, I tried whatever I could to increase my chances and earn a living. I studied for an insurance license, managed to pass the exam, and tried to sell insurance and financial securities. Again, I ran into the situation of not being able to drive and learned a very difficult lesson. Even though people might have volunteered to drive me around when I needed to go, they soon got tired of it. I learned very quickly you do not go by your own schedule. You must go only when others are willing to take you. My great savior was my music. I was still able to tune pianos, my wife had a job, and we were able to keep our heads somewhat above water, although I found myself in my mid-50s and becoming quite depressed because I was not earning as the bread winner.

In 1990, a small music store in our town became available for sale. I used to visit that music store regularly, almost every day, while I was essentially unemployed. One day, I walked in and the owner said, "I'm thinking of selling the store. Do you know anybody who would be interested?" I looked at him and said, "Hell no. How much do you want for it?" He gave me a price, we discussed it, and we negotiated a bit. I came home and told my wife that we had a chance to buy a music store, but of course we had no money. My mother-in-law then spoke up and said, "I will give you the money to buy the store." It was around $30,000.00. We bought the store.

May 1, 1990 was a bright sunny day, with blue skies and warm weather. I got up early that morning, ate break-fast, kissed my wife goodbye, walked out of the house, and started the three-block journey from my home to the music store. The previous owner was there when I arrived having agreed to spend a few days with me to help me get used to the inventory and the daily routines of operating the store. I approached it with a great deal of hope. I had five years of struggling to find a way to make a living. My first day at the store was kind of a disappointment. I continued piano tuning and teaching guitar lessons at our new store as we sold instruments but need to also mention that my wife taught piano and played organ in the church we attended at that time. We took in exactly $29.00 in sales that day. I left the store at 5:00 pm wondering if I had made a big mistake. The next day was Sunday, which gave me a lot of time to think. Monday morning came and I started in again. This was the beginning of a new adventure.

In the course of my first couple of years with the store, we were located in a basement underneath what was formerly a JJ Newberry department store. The building had been purchased by a private person that sectioned it off so that there could be several businesses located there. In the basement with my store, there was a tax collection office, a small restaurant, a hair salon, and a sports equipment shop. As time passed during my first few months owning the store, other businesses in the basement with me began to fail. The restaurant changed hands and then went out of business. The tax office was relocated. The sports shop went out of business. Before long, I was the only store left

in the basement of that old JJ Newberry building. I began
to question if the location wasn't a bad one.

In 1994, We decided that we would try for a new location and found one on the main street in downtown. The
rent was reasonable and so, with the help of some of my best
customers and my cousin, we moved the store in one day over
a weekend. We were open in the old location on a Saturday
and opened that following Monday at the new location.

Music N' More, December 2019

30 years have now come and gone since the day we opened our little music store and I see no end to it. We've changed locations to a better position in town and we've also had changes over the years in what we sell in the store. At 82 years old, I still teach guitar, banjo, mandolin, and bass guitar. My wife still teaches piano and today has more than 50 students. She continues to play organ for the church we currently go to. We've managed to carve out a rather good living in music, even though we were both told as young people that we would never be able to do so unless we got a degree in music education and served as a band or choir director in the public-school system. Neither one of us felt we wanted to do that.

Chapter 15: The Store and Friends

Scott

During my time in the music store, I have met some fascinating people. They all started out as customers or friends of the business and turned into personal friends. One of the earliest ones I met was a young man named Scott. He was a high school senior when we first met. He liked guitar and one of the functions at my store was giving guitar lessons. Scott had come in with the idea of improving his guitar playing ability. I soon learned that my social work skills were quite useful in this endeavor. When dealing with a client in social work, the idea is to get the client to trust you, believe in you, or put another way, to sell yourself. I found that's exactly what one has to do in business; sell himself. That is probably more important than the selling of a product. Scott, in addition to learning guitar, was having some problems deciding what to do after school. His parents had a business and his father, who was getting older, wanted him to take over the business when he finished college. Scott had been accepted at a small university not far from the store and as part of his admission, he was asked to write a paper about someone who had been influential in his life. He was to write the essay and submit it in a competition for a scholarship that was awarded by the president of the college. He asked if he could submit an essay based on his relationship with me. I said yes.

He submitted the essay and I learned that he won the contest. He was awarded several thousands of dollars scholarship that assisted him in paying for his college education. I never saw the essay. He never showed it to me. To this day, I have no idea what he wrote, but I'm certainly happy for Scott. He remained a good friend for a long time after and when he graduated from college, he came to me again. He said that he felt guilty because unlike many of his fellow graduates, he already had a job and could be in his father's business. I assured him that he should not feel guilty and that most any father who had a business would be pleased as punch to have a child of his take over when he was ready to retire.

Tim

One of the other people I met and who has remained a long-time friend in the music business is Tim. I don't recall when he came in the store for the first time or how many times he visited before I caught on that he was a regular. Tim was an older gentleman. Probably in his 40s at that time. He was a mail carrier for the post office. Tim was also a pretty good guitar player. He played in a praise band for a mega-church in our area. As we became acquainted, I learned that Tim's mother was a neighbor of mine when we lived in the little community called Greenburr during my early years. She had actually babysat me at one time. As our relationship developed, I learned that Tim could do certain repairs. He was a very handy individual. He fixed his own cars. He did a lot of work around his own house and was quite good at rewiring guitars. He was an excellent worker as a result of an earlier job he had with a furniture company.

Tim is still one of my good friends. He comes into the shop once every week and does work that I may have for him that I don't feel capable of doing myself. He's helped me in many ways over the years, not just with the store but as a good friend. Every Tuesday night he drives me home. My kids don't call me Tuesday evenings because they know it's "Tim Time." He hauls away all of my excess cardboard and helps take care of various things around the store. He never takes money for the work he does for me. Tim and I have a bit of a bartering arrangement. He fills up over time what he likes to call, "Store credit," which eventually

I honor when Tim finds something I have in the shop that he likes. One of the great jokes between us is a guitar that Tim now owns. He ordered a guitar from me way back in the 1990s. He eventually traded it in on something else that he wanted. Later on, he came back and traded to receive the guitar he originally ordered again. He and I have traded this very guitar back and forth probably five times over the course of several years. It's a guitar that he and I decided will never be owned by anybody but him or me.

Josey

There's also Josey. She's a teen-aged girl who has studied guitar for the past three years and has become quite an excellent player. One day last year, Josey had come to me and said that she and her mother wanted to decorate my store for Christmas. I explained I couldn't because of not being able to climb around on ladders and reach higher places. Josey said I was not to worry about that. She and her mother would make Christmas decorations and see to it that the store was nicely decorated for the Holidays. The two of them made Christmas decorations out of guitar picks. The also took guitar strings and made garlands for a little Christmas tree. Josey's mother, who is quite artistic, made snowflakes out of music staff paper. The two of them hung the musically themed decorations all throughout the store along with gobs and gobs of Christmas lights. They must have spent four or five hours decorating the store, never mind the amount of time they spent procuring the materials and making everything. They also assured me that I would not be left with the happy task of tearing down the decorations at the end of the season and sure enough, they came back and did so for me. We kept the decorations and they told me as long as I have the store, they will come and decorate it each year.

You can see from my brief passages about Scott, Tim, and Josey, that in fact have made close friends out of a number of customers over the years and have become almost like family. They're regulars, they come in, we talk, they buy things, and I sell things. Most shop owners would probably be appalled that I put my customers to work and in fact, I do many times. Frequently when they ask for something and I fail to find it because I forgot where I put it, they many times will find it for me. I have customers who come in to buy parts. Rather than me going fishing for parts, I open the bin and tell them to find what they want, put on the counter and pay for it. When my granddaughters come to visit, I often put them to work running the vacuum. Of course, I give them something for doing it. This is the kind of shop I run and I'm very proud of it.

I have no plans of retiring. I love what I do. I feel secure in it and will keep doing it as long as I can. I have a philosophy of business that says, "Be fair to your customers and they will be fair to you." I don't make money my major goal. I feel that if I give good and honest service, the money will come, and indeed it does,

Chapter 16: Barbara

I came to work in the Lewisburg area in August 1977. I had been at the agency for about two weeks when I was finally introduced to the last staff member I had to meet. She had been on vacation when I came to work there. I was introduced, given her name, and said hello to her. She said in response, "Hi." She walked into her office and slammed the door behind her. I thought this was a strange reaction but overlooked it and went on from there. It soon became clear to me that the person I just met didn't want anything to do with me. She barely spoke to me. Matters were made worse when the director of the agency suggested that she drive around and show me the various places we did business with, including some residential facilities for the mentally retarded and some other facilities with a focus on mental health.

About four weeks after we had met, the staff was invited to dinner at one of the staff members houses. We were scheduled to have an evening meeting at the agency later that night. We went to dinner and conversation lead from one thing to another. The staff and hostess asked me, "Do you still tune pianos?" Suddenly, this woman who wanted little to do with me said, "You tune pianos?" I told her I did. She asked me if I would teach her how to tune them. I said no. She asked why I wouldn't. I said, "First of all, I don't even know if you have an ear for tuning pianos. Secondly, you have no tools. Thirdly, we have no pianos and it's going to require some time." Her answer to me was, "I have money. I can buy tools. I have time since I'm single and I can get us pianos." She also informed me that she was an accomplished pianist.

Three days went by and finally she came and knocked on my office door. She said, "I have seven pianos. Do you think that's enough to get started to learn how to tune?" I told her that it was. Every evening we went out and we tuned pianos. I did the tuning and showed her some of how to do it. I was paid for the piano tunings. They kept coming. One day one of my colleagues at the agency said to me, "You realize that you are dating this woman?" I said, "No I'm not. I'm going piano tuning and she's driving." My colleague replied by saying, "Well, the fact is that you are dating her." So, as I like to tell people when they ask me how we met, ours was a situation which degenerated into a friendship, degenerated from a friendship into a romance, and then degenerated from a romance into a marriage. Barbara and

I were married May 19, 1979. We have now been married for over 41 years. She teaches piano and I still work at the store teaching other instruments as well as selling various musical items.

We continued for the next five years to work in the business of mental health for the same counseling agency. She was a caseworker working with the mentally retarded as they were called then. I was a therapist and supervisor working in mental health. By 1984 and 1985, we had decided that we had had enough of the mental health and mental retardation situation. Funding was tight. We were asked to do ridiculous things in order to meet bureaucratic obligations, which continued to grow. This interfered with our capability to do good counseling work with the patients who came in.

In 1980, Barbara decided to launch a new career in piano teaching while she was still working in mental health. She enrolled into Temple University's Harrisburg extension in a Master of Social Work program. For a year, from 1980 to 1981, she was teaching piano, working full time and traveling back and forth to Harrisburg once a week in order to meet her MSW course obligations. By 1981, however, she admitted a personal discovery. She told me, "Social work is not for me. It is not what I want to do."

I replied, "I agree. It's not for you. Don't do it." She left the graduate school program having completed one full year with solid A grades.

Her first student as a piano teacher was a local oral surgeon. A few weeks later, he enrolled his daughters into taking piano lessons and her career as a piano teacher began. She continued to do other work with a mental retardation facility in the area on a part-time basis after leaving the mental health clinic. Her piano teaching business grew, and in a few years, she built a business, which included more than fifty students each week. This required a great deal of work on her part. Later, she also took on the responsibility in our church as the organist. The previous organist had left for health reasons. She served in that capacity until 2001 when a new pastor came to the church who didn't like the organ and made it abundantly clear that he wanted contemporary music with guitars and drums and the like. This was not our idea of good solid sacred church music. She left her organist job at the church but continued her piano teaching.

Our lives were complicated even further in 1993 when Barbara's mother suffered a stroke at the age of eighty-two. She had been living independently in an apartment twelve miles away from us. After having treatment for the stroke, her doctor informed us that she should not live alone. Because of her generosity in helping us to purchase the music store, I said to Barb, "We need to give her a home in our home." And we did. She lived with us for eight years until she passed away from ovarian cancer in 2001 at the age of eighty-nine. She had been helpful in many ways.

She assisted in preparing for meals. She often read interesting newspaper articles to me each night when I would come home from work that she thought I would be interested in. She was a good patient. She followed what her doctors told her to do and cooperated in every way. I used to go pick up her prescriptions at a local drugstore since Barbara was busy with her piano teaching business and her organist business and other things as well.

Since 2001, we have lived our lives in a rather simple fashion. We're not great travelers; we enjoy our home, and our hobby happens to be the rearing of dogs. In a course of getting treatment for one of our dogs at a local veterinarian, we met an individual who introduced us to her mother. She raised and showed white west-highland terriers. We had purchased a terrier from a pet shop, and he died in 2001. We were concerned about where we would find somebody who rears such animals. This person turned out to be quite an interesting woman in her own right. She was a professional singer; her dogs had served in commercials and had seen them without knowing they were hers. We then adopted every time she retired a white west-highland from show business even after the dog had puppies and had completed his or her championships to earn their show quality status. She choose to retire them rather than kill them or abandon them. We became a white west highland terrier retirement center and at one time had as many as seven. Today, we have three.

Barbara has been my major support and encourager for the past forty years. She is the kind of person who attends to detail. I am the sort of person who often comes up with ideas, but seldom follow through and figure out all the details. Barbara's the one who asks the questions after I let her know what the ideas are. She has been very good at keeping me on a straight track. She stuck with ideas I could do something with and develop into a success. She has also been very good at helping me to decide to discard certain ideas in which I don't have a chance. We have been married for over forty-one years and I hope we stay married for at least another forty-one.

Dick and Barb, May 2018

Letters to my children

Chapter 17: Prejudice Towards the Blind

Most people, once they find out about my visual problems, have one of two extreme reactions. As I talk to them about how I make my living they either express amazement or they tend to believe I am not capable of much. Talking with other blind and partially sighted friends, I find that they have similar experiences as me. They also express in blind school there was no room for racial prejudice. It was minimal if it occurred at all. One reason is blind or partially sighted people have also experienced our share of discrimination. Imagine what it's like to go into a grocery store and not be able to read the label of anything on the shelves, or what it's like to have to go someplace and not be able to drive in order to get there. Imagine what it's like to not be able to see a traffic light or what it is like to not be able to find your way around in a restaurant. I have friends who had guide dogs and even though the law says that these service animals must be allowed in restaurants, or on airplanes and such, people have frequently experienced not being permitted to allow the dogs in. One friend of mine tells the story of how she was flying from Washington, DC to North Carolina with her guide dog. She was flying coach. One of the passengers complained about having a dog on the airplane. The passenger called for one of the flight attendants and insisted that something be done about the dog on the airplane. The airline was brilliant! They took my friend and her guide dog and sat them up in first class seating.

Another friend of mine that had a guide dog experienced going into a restaurant and was told she couldn't come in with her dog, even though the law lets service dogs in public places. She was asked to leave. She raised the question of the law allowing service animals to come in but was still ordered to leave the restaurant. She became so angry that she contacted the local newspaper and submitted an article about the attitude of the restaurant. The restaurant owner lost his business license for violating the law. Even though this is law, we have to fight to have the law honored.

I remember while I was at Penn State, I had at least one reader that indicated that if I could not do my own reading and so forth, I shouldn't be there, even though the state government paid my way. I finally grew angry with this reaction and said, "You, my reader, are worse off than I am. You're ignorant!" Perhaps this discriminatory behavior from others is why we have some sympathy for some people in minorities who also experience substantial discriminations. The blind and partially sighted don't have any politically powerful groups advocating for us. There is the Americans with Disabilities Act, but it is another act in which there are many violations. Even the government commits violations of this act. It's not a pleasant experience to have this kind of discrimination thrown at you. As a child, I can remember being called names such as Four Eyes and the Blind Bat from Pittsburgh because of my thick Coke bottle glasses and my jumpy eyes.

Discrimination is real and it will probably always be around in some form. Discrimination towards the blind goes as far back as Biblical times. Remember the story of Bartolomeus, the blind man Jesus cured outside of the temple. Bartolomeus was so de-statused in his society that he didn't have a name. Bartolomeus simply means the son of Tolomeus. It is not the blind man's name. He was not even permitted to go into the temple or participate in any form of his society, yet when he regained his sight, his whole world changed. It is not surprising that blind people through the centuries were forced to begging in the streets. Ultimately, the law against begging was passed and in order to circumvent the law, blind people for many years bypassed it by selling pencils so they could receive money on the streets.

I can remember an incident when I first got the music store, and a customer came in who happened to be a college professor. He suggested to me that I should take my guitar and tin cup and sit out on the street and play music for money. I mentioned that we were making serious effort to avoid and eliminate that kind of image. He later called me and apologized. I told him that I accepted his apology and that I knew of more ways to make fun of myself than what he could ever think of. When I first went to work in the mental health field, I had been at one particular job for about three months, and the staff psychiatrist who was the medical director called me into his office and said, "I want to tell you that I used to work with a totally blind psychologist in another facility. I considered her to be no good and not worth the trouble it took to have her there. When I heard that you had interviewed for this job, I was against hiring you. I was wrong." On the one hand, I felt complimented and I felt respected in that he had at least been honest enough to tell me what his feelings were. He did not have to do that. On the other hand, here's a man, a physician, who's a trained professional in the business of helping people, working with people of various handicaps, saying that he had no faith on a prejudicial basis. He had never met me or interviewed me. I had to interview for that particular job three times. This was not in agreement with the laws in that I had to have civil service qualifications through the state of PA to interview for the job. The law said that if I interviewed for the job, if I was available to take the job, and that there was no other contestant for the job, they had to hire me. I was asked to come back for three different interviews. The last interview happened in front of about 20 people: the entire staff of the agency and the board of directors. They asked ridiculous questions and the one that was finally the straw that broke the camel's back was, "What is your philosophy of life?" Thoroughly annoyed with the whole situation, I answered the person who asked the question by saying, "It's taken me over 40 years to develop it. I don't think I can tell it to you in five minutes." I then said I had enough of interviews. "If you don't want to hire me, say so and I'm gone. If you have no reason not to hire me, give me the job." There was no answer. I got up and walked out of the interview. Suddenly, the administrator of mental health came out after me and said, "You Have the job. You have the job. You have the job." I told him that my experience thus far left me with a bad impression of the agency and that I wasn't sure I wanted it. He told me that they were desperate to hire me so I finally said to them, "I'll give it three months and we will see how it goes. If I'm not happy, I won't stay."

This is the kind of behavior that not only I but others like me have had to endure throughout their lives. It's unpleasant, it's unnecessary, and it creates a great deal of anger. I have become a person with a somewhat fighting spirit because of this. I anticipate that at any new situation, it's very likely I will have to fight in order to be recognized for what my capabilities are. As one individual who worked with me for a long period of time said, "Working with you is like arm wrestling."

Chapter 18: 20/20 Vision

Most of my life I have been asked if I miss the notion of having 20/20 vision. I've never had perfect sight, so I don't know what I'm missing. People who have been blinded after birth would understand what it is like to have 20/20 vision. I don't miss having good vision because I've never experienced it. I never lost anything. This is my normal. There are two or three experiences throughout my life in which the issue of, "Wouldn't you rather have 20/20 vision," had come up. In 1969, Linda's mother pulled her aside and spoke to her about an article she had read in the Reader's Digest. It was about an ophthalmologist at Yale University who had invented a contact lens which restored full vision to many of his low vision patients. Linda's mother thought I should go try this new lens, but she did not speak to me directly about it. She offered to pay for the lenses and our trip to Connecticut to try them out. Linda spoke to me about it and was enthusiastic. Linda wished for me to have 20/20 vision. She suggested that if her mother was willing to pay for it, perhaps I should go try it. I decided to play along. We piled into our 1968 Mercury Park Lane and drove to Fairfield,

CT. We met with our doctor who happened to be chairman of the ophthalmology department at Yale University. He described the lenses he created. They were called Scalaral Lenses. The lenses covered the entire eye unlike the usual contact lens. The concept was there would be no therapeutic gap between the eye and the lens like with glasses or typical contact lenses. The lens would be as close to natural as possible and would restore greater vision. The fitting for the lens was an experience I will never forget.

I laid down on a table with fluorescent lights above me. The doctor explained to me that I needed to lie perfectly still and not move a muscle. He then filled my right eye with a plastic cup, like an inverted hourglass. As I lay there with the hourglass covering my entire eye, a green gelatinous liquid came down from the top of the glass and filled my entire right eye. It was cold and I could not move. I did not like the thought of having to repeat the entire process if I did move as he stated. After the green gelatinous substance was in my eye for some time, I felt the slithering of a knife going around the edges of my eye cutting away the excess material. After five minutes, the doctor pulled on the hourglass and the entire glass along with a mold of my eye came out. The procedure was then repeated on my left eye. The doctor assured me that my performance had been good and there was no need to repeat the procedure. From these molds, my Scalaral Lenses would be made. It would take another two weeks before they were ready.

We returned to Connecticut to see the doctor in his office and he fitted the Scalaral Lenses. He asked me what the result was. I told him that my vision was not changed. It was actually worse. The glasses that I normally wear have bifocals which allow for an increase of vision in the lower section of my visual field. The doctor was disappointed and frustrated. I told him that he should not worry about it. I lost nothing. I was accustomed to my vision the way it was, and I was not horribly disappointed. I was surprised at my own reaction, especially since everybody seemed to be wishing for me to have 20/20 vision. The Scalaral Lenses proved to be difficult. I tried them for a couple of months. I could only wear them for a short period of time. Film would build up under the lens and in my eye, which caused pain, visual difficulty, and swelling. I took the Scalaral Lenses and put them away and went back to using my glasses. My glasses were normal for me. I never heard directly from Linda's mother what her feelings were. I know she was disappointed that I did not get 20/20 vision even though I wasn't.

A second incident occurred with the visual business in 1987. I was out of work and had contacted the Pennsylvania

Bureau of Vocational Rehabilitation to help me find employment. They decided I needed some visual enhancement. They fitted me with a pair of glasses which had a telescopic lens on the one side called a Bioptic Scope. I have always referred to it as my bionic eye, like the popular show, "The Six Million Dollar Man," with Lee Majors as the bionic man. I was fitted with the Bioptic Scope for my right eye because my left eye is virtually useless. I discovered that I had, through a very narrow field of vision, 20/30 vision. I've never experienced this before. I remember standing on the street corner waiting to cross the street. I looked to my right and there was a car virtually on top of me. I looked to my left and there were cars seemingly just passed that were almost on top of me. Nothing was the same. Everything appeared larger, closer, and more detailed. I was not accustomed to seeing things this way. When my wife and I went to a mall shopping, I discovered that I couldn't stand it. My eyes were hit with the amazing number of lights, flashing signs, and all kinds of stimulation I wasn't used to. My brain seemed unable to handle it. I found myself getting very anxious and upset.

I was fascinated to some degree with what I was able to see through the scope. I remember seeing fog through the scope and wondering exactly what that was. It didn't look anything like fog did to me. I also remember looking at signs with pictures of deer running on them and asked Barb, "What is that?" She explained that it was a sign warning of deer crossing. I enjoyed reading mileage signs along Interstate 80 when we drove. I enjoyed reading stop signs and exit signs ahead. I couldn't read them fully because I'm not accustomed to fast reading. It was an experience but was more disruptive than helpful.

The Bioptic Scope was heavy. I was wearing a pair of glasses that were light and normal on one side, and very heavy on the other side. The result was after wearing it for a while, I would get blistering headaches. It became clear to me that I was not a fan of the Bioptic Scope. Life was not normal to me. Finally, I took it off in frustration and never wore it again. I realized, to my amazement, I was well adjusted to the way things were and did not wish to have 20/20 vision. At least I had a glimpse of what it would be like. It was not pleasant for me. I am certain that full-sighted people will probably have difficulty understanding this as they read it, but that's the way it is.

Letters to my children

Chapter 19: Gestalt

Since early childhood, people have asked me, "What's it like to be blind? How much can you see?" That's a difficult question to answer. I can see long distances, what some people call farsighted. I can't tell you detail in the distances I see. Most of what I see is not in the detail that others do. I learned this firsthand when I tried the Bioptic Scope and had 20/30 vision in a narrow field out of my right eye. I realized how much detail fully sighted people see and how little detail I see. I draw conclusions on things I see based on minimal detail. Remember the incident of the purple coat? This is a good example. I saw the purple coat and from that assumed it was the woman who was my friend that always teased me. I ended up being wrong and that happens sometimes.

We can make really horrible decisions sometimes based on minimal detail. Most of the time my inferences are correct. They're based on life experiences. It's important for me to organize things and keep them in a specific order in my memory. My clothing, for example, I usually hang my shirts in a specific order so that I know what color is in what place. Most people with low vision or total blindness have

to keep track of the environment all of the time by knowing where things are, how long ago this or that happened,
what is around you, and what are all of the sounds you
hear. This is the only way someone with limited sight or
no vision can orient himself to person and place. This is a
great energy consumer. Keeping track of the environment
at all times takes a great deal of effort and a great amount
of concentration. I will show you an example of Gestalt with
the following drawing:

Example of Gestalt

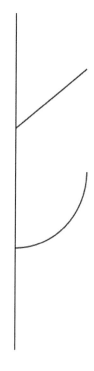

I have asked you to infer a picture from the drawing on the previous page. The picture being a corner of a building and a soldier around the corner with his dog. The dog's tail is sticking out at the lower right and the soldier's gun sticking out at the upper part of the drawing. This is what is Gestalt. It implies finishing a concept on the basis of a minimal amount of detail.

Often, young children will ask me about my thick glasses or my jumpy eyes. Their parents usually scold them and try to pull them away out of embarrassment. Over the years I have learned to tell parents that they should not be embarrassed. Their children are simply asking an honest question and deserve an honest answer. I explain to them that I need the thick glasses in order to see better and that I have the jumpy eyes because of the multiple operations performed on my eyes when I was a baby. This usually satisfies the children's curiosity, and they forget about it.

I have to try to explain how much I can see by virtue of the fact that people think I seem to get around well, I have very good vision. Many people who don't know me misjudge and think I have 20/20 vision until I make a mistake in judgement. They find themselves surprised. A good friend of mine who is also partially blind told me a story of how he was waiting for a specific bus in the city.

He was in line at the bus stop. When the bus pulled up, he was not certain of its number. He moved ahead in the line to see what the number was and if it was the numbered bus he was to use for travel. He was immediately castigated by all of the people in the line since they didn't realize he couldn't read the number unless he walked up close. Because he had some vision and was familiar with the territory, they assumed that he had 20/20 vision. They were surprised he did not have 20/20 vision. This is what often happens to people with partial vision.

The public has the idea or notion that you are either blind, which means you can't see anything, or that you are sighted, which means you are fully sighted. They do not understand the concept of varying shades of gray ranging from total darkness all the way to total light. They don't understand the idea that sight is on a continuum. It is a matter of degree and its variable from person to person. My wife is often troubled by the fact that I seem able to see some things normally and other things she thinks I should be able to see, I cannot. After 41 years of marriage, she says she still does not understand exactly how my vision operates. I have to remind her I can't explain. It's simply the way things are.

Chapter 20: Closing

Now you have it. Of course, many things have happened to your father in the course of his life, which are not included in this book. But hopefully this has been a cross section and enough information to let you know who your father is, what he did, how he has lived and how he is now. I am about to enter my eighty-third year of life and eighty-three years is a great deal to cover. I don't think it can be done for anybody in one book. Hopefully, this gives you some insights into who I am, what I did and how things turned out.

As I look back on my life and reflect, trying to figure out what big meaning I can take from all of these 80+ years, it occurs to me that whether I am doing social work, whether I am teaching instruments, or whether I am doing a sermon or a service at church, all of my behavior comes down to one activity; I am a teacher. First, last and foremost. All these activities involve teaching. Over the years, I have had many students. Likewise, Barb has also had many students. She too is a teacher. We have been rewarded as teachers by the successes of many of our students. Some have gone on to be doctors. Some have gone on to be finance counselors.

Some have gone on to be attorneys. And yes, some have even gone on to careers in music. At least one of my wife's students has received a PHD and teaches at a rather prestigious eastern school of music. Two of my students are now performing country music musicians in Nashville. Several others have gone on to perform in garage bands and, if they don't study music and make a career of it, they at least keep it as a hobby.

We often have fleeting contacts of students who tell us what's happening in their lives. Every teacher wants to see their students turn out better than they. That's also true of every parent. In fact, parents at their best are teachers. They teach their children the things they need to become adults and survive on their own. I don't know how much I've been involved in your teaching, but I hope somewhat. And I hope that I've had a hand in some of your successes.

Thank you for your indulgence and I hope my letters are meaningful to you.

With love, Your Dad

Rick and Cindy all grown up

Acknowledgments

Many people have helped me with this project. Both directly and indirectly. I first want to give a special thank you to my son Rick and my daughter Cindy for all of their help and encouragement. A special thank you also to my wife Barbara for her support and inspiration.

Many others, too numerous to mention, have offered their praise for me to write this book, including my mother, both of my brothers, nieces and nephews, and others who are simply good friends. A special thanks to all of you.

Charles R. Bressler

Dick at 82 years young

CPSIA information can be obtained
at www.ICGtesting.com
Printed in the USA
BVHW020655060221
599517BV00029B/353

9 781662 907609